Afghan Hound

by Bryony Harcourt-Brown

Table of Contents

PUBLISHED IN THE
UNITED KINGDOM BY:

INTERPET
P U B L I S H I N G

Vincent Lane, Dorking
Surrey RH4 3YX
England

ISBN 1-902389-08-5

92
Housebreaking and Training Your Afghan Hound

by Charlotte Schwartz
Be informed about the importance of training your Afghan Hound from the basics of housebreaking and understanding the development of a young dog to executing obedience commands (sit, stay, down, etc.).

PHOTO CREDITS:

Norvia Behling
TJ Calhoun
Carolina Biological Supply
Doskocil
Isabelle Francais
James Hayden-Yoav
James R Hayden, RBP
Bill Jonas
Alice van Kempen

Dwight R Kuhn
Dr Dennis Kunkel
Mikki Pet Products
Phototake
Jean Claude Revy
Alice Roche
Steven Sourifman
Dr Andrew Spielman
Bryony Trafford

Illustrations by Renee Low.

The author would like to thank Dr Malcolm Willis for information supplied regarding hip displasia.

119
Health Care of Your Afghan Hound

Discover how to select a proper veterinary surgeon and care for your dog at all stages of life. Topics include vaccination scheduling, skin problems, dealing with external and internal parasites and the medical and behavioural conditions common to the breed.

146
Showing Your Afghan Hound

Experience the dog show world, including different types of shows and the making up of a champion. Go beyond the conformation ring to working trials and agility trials, etc.

Copyright © 2000 Animalia, Ltd.
Cover patent pending. Printed in Korea.

The Afghan Hound is one of the most beautiful and graceful, as well as one of the fastest, dogs known in the world of canines.

HISTORY OF THE
AFGHAN HOUND

The Afghan Hound is a unique and noble breed that traces its ancestry back through history as a dog bred for strength of limb and soundness of movement. These

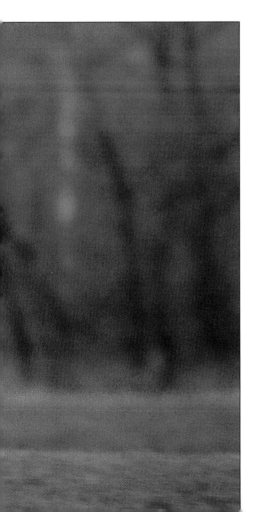

dogs are fleet of foot and capable of dramatic turns of speed when running. The Afghan Hound is a sighthound, that is to say a dog that hunts by sight and not scent, as opposed to a scenthound such as the Bloodhound. The Afghan Hound will frequently survey the far horizon with an intent stare, appearing to see objects that humans find out of their range of vision. The hunting instinct is still present in some Afghan Hounds; small game such as rabbits is of particular interest to an Afghan Hound in the mood for fun and allowed to indulge himself.

The typical Afghan Hound is a most amazing dog, unique in so many aspects of its physical and mental being. For those who love and understand the breed, having once lived with an Afghan Hound it is hard to find another breed that matches the companionship of one of these dogs.

ORIGINS OF THE BREED

Afghan Hounds were originally found in Afghanistan, a country of extremes in both terrain and temperature. The similarities of the Afghan Hound to the Saluki,

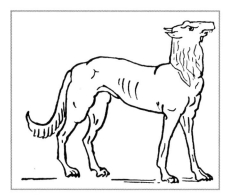

The Albanian Wolfhound was known in ancient times as a fierce, fast and extremely ferocious breed that was used in hunting and protection. This illustration derives from an ancient Greek vase.

in both body and head, have led to the belief held by many experts that the Saluki was the forefather of the Afghan Hound. Both breeds have been likened to Greyhounds, the Afghan Hound actually having been called Persian Greyhound, historically.

In the canine history of Afghanistan, various hound-type breeds seem to have been popular amongst the indigenous peoples. Over time, various strains, which were used for various types of hunting, are reputed to have formed; these dogs were often collectively referred to as Tazis. Early Afghan Hounds became highly prized for their qualities as hunting companions.

DID YOU KNOW?

Having been impressed by the breed when on a film location in Britain, Zeppo Marx (of the Marx brothers) and his wife imported a pair of cream hounds to America in the 1930s.

One can only wonder at the impression that these wild and independent hounds must have made on Westerners who were lucky enough to have seen them in their own territory. These dogs, so fleet of foot and dramatic in demeanour, must have appeared most amazing creatures to people seeing them for the first time. The coat pattern, with the short coat on the face, back and pasterns and the long silky coat on the top-knot, ears, body, legs and feet, coupled with the beautiful expressive head, must have left a lasting memory.

THE AFGHAN HOUND GOES TO BRITAIN

Despite a number of imports into Britain, from as early as the 1880s, the first dog to really make a major impression on the British dog-showing fraternity was Zardin, who came to the country in the early 1900s. Zardin was successful in the ring and was widely commended, to such an extent that he was used as the model for the Afghan Hound breed standard, the revised version of which is still used as the blueprint by which Afghan Hounds are judged today.

The next major event in the history of Afghan Hounds in Britain began in the 1920s with the return from Baluchistan of Major Bell-Murray and his family. Major Bell-Murray had acquired a number of Afghan Hounds, over a period of time, whilst still living in India on the Afghanistan border. One of his original Afghans was Begum, a self-masked (that is, the face the same as the overall colour of the dog) white/cream bitch.

Also living in India around this time was Mrs Amps, whilst her husband Major Amps was in Kabul. Major Amps acquired a male Afghan Hound for his wife, who showed the dog in India. Other Afghan Hounds were obtained by Major Amps to build up the foundation of the Ghazni kennel.

Major and Mrs Amps returned to Britain with their Afghan Hounds in the mid-1920s. In

DID YOU KNOW?

Afghan Hounds have a reputation for being known as the 'scented hound'. This is due to another remarkable

phenomenon of the breed, the production of a scent from glands on the sides of the cheeks. The scent is quite intoxicating on dogs that carry it to its most concentrated level, especially when the dog is damp. The pleasant scent is a musk-like smell and adds yet another facet of interest to these wonderful hounds.

At the turn of the 20th century, the Afghan Hound was known as the Barukhzy. The name was taken from the name of the royal family of Afghanistan. Mrs M Wood's Westmall Tamasar, shown here, shows the typical head of the breed at that time.

kennels, the Bell-Murrays' being longer of leg, finer of head and sparser of coat, and the Ghazni dogs being stockier, more heavily coated and stronger in head. These differences in type led to some friction amongst devotees of the Afghan Hound at the time and, for long after this, Afghan Hounds would regularly be labelled as being of either Ghazni or Bell-Murray type, predominantly according to their coat patterns and heads. No definite confirmation has ever really been given denoting the correctness of either type and both have merit in different ways. Today both these types have been merged, due to breeders bringing both strains together in their breeding programmes. However, occasionally, puppies are still born within litters that show quite obvious resemblance to either

Britain, the Amps' hounds continued to be registered under the kennel name of Ghazni. It is thought that the Ghazni hounds mainly originated from the more mountainous regions of Afghanistan around Kabul, whereas the Bell-Murray hounds reputedly came more from the plains or desert areas around the border of Afghanistan with India. There were differences in type between the dogs of the two

This dog dating from 1888 was selected as the best type of dog that an Afghan Hound could be. It is interesting to compare to modern-day dogs.

DID YOU KNOW?

In 1901 Mrs Whitbread presented the body of the deceased Afghan Hound Shahzada to the British Museum, where it has been preserved.

Bell-Murray or Ghazni breeding. This was even more in evidence when we acquired our first Afghan Hound, in the 1960s, as she strongly resembled the Bell-Murray type.

The first Afghan Hound champion in Britain was Ch Buckmal, bred by Major Bell-Murray and owned by Miss Manson. Ch Sirdar of Ghazni was a highly influential early Afghan who won eight Challenge Certificates (three are required to obtain the title of Champion in Britain). Sirdar is reputed to have possessed a more outgoing and friendly temperament than the Bell-Murray hounds, which were reputedly more aloof and distant. It seems, however, that not all the Ghazni hounds were dissimilar to the Bell-Murray type, with some of the long-legged and lighter-coated variety. By the 1930s, both of these famous kennels were no longer active in Britain, with Mrs Amps suffering from ill health. The Bell-Murray hounds, in the hands of Miss Manson, originally the Bell-Murrays' governess, and under the kennel name of Cove, visited America.

Despite other imports over this period by, amongst others, Miss Bowring, the Bell-Murray and Ghazni strains were to form the main lines in Britain. Over the following years many other people were to enter the network of Afghan devotees, with such

famous kennels making their mark as Geufron, Acklam, Ainsdart, Westmill, Jalalabad, el Kabul, Chaman, Turkuman and other famous names. The Chaman kennel of Miss Molly Sharpe was a particularly influential kennel and was successful in surviving the war years, a considerable feat, due to dogs from the Chaman kennel travelling to live in Ireland, with their owners, and some being exported to America.

In the post-war era, many new

Afghan Hound

In Hutchinson's *Dog Encyclopaedia*, the Afghan Hound was compared to the Saluki and described as 'larger and stronger and with a much heavier coat.'

names came into the breed, including the Bletchingly, Netheroyd, Patrols, Khorrassan and Carloway, Barakzai, Barbille and Khanabad kennels. These influential kennels were respon-

sible for many of the famous dogs of the time, which have shaped the history of the breed and the background of our present-day Afghan Hounds.

From small numbers at its outset of popularity, the Afghan Hound quickly gained in strength of numbers. The 1970s saw a major population explosion and the production of large numbers of puppies to meet the ever-increasing demand. The result of this was that these highly individual dogs were exposed to a huge variety of homes, many of which they were entirely unsuited

DID YOU KNOW?

The arguments between the devotees of the Bell-Murray-type hounds that were taller, of slighter build and sparser of coat and those of the Ghazni type, which were of heavier build and coat, were to cause much controversy over many years.

14

to and which were unsuitable for them. From this time, although widely recognised, not to say considered commonplace, the Afghan Hound was nevertheless widely misunderstood. The tide eventually turned and the Afghan Hound population reduced to a much more realistic level. Nevertheless, the breed still continued to do well in the show ring, with two Crufts Best in Show winners: Mrs Pauline Gibbs' Ch Montravia Kaskarak Hitari in 1983 and Mr and Mrs Chris and Julie Amoo's Ch Viscount Grant in 1987.

The early 1960s saw the first import of American stock into Britain. These included the controversial Ch Wazir of Desertaire. Wazir was a very influential dog in the history of the breed in Britain and appeared to shape some of the feelings of British Afghan breeders towards American stock until very recently. The legacy he left included some well-liked attributes such as an outgoing, human-loving temperament and strength of topline, and also some less well-liked features in head, shoulders and tail, for instance.

Nowadays a healthier attitude towards imports seems to exist, and one would hope that the general trend will be towards the breeding of excellent specimens irrespective of their country of

The Afghan Hound as it is known today is not the ideal dog for every household. Afghans can be aloof and difficult to train, but they are loveable, loyal and active and, therefore, attractive to certain people.

DID YOU KNOW?

Early Afghan Hound temperaments reputedly ranged from the extremely shy hound, nervous of unknown people and places to those known for their aggressive traits. Nowadays these

excessive variations of temperament have largely been bred out of the breed. However, stories of the strength of the bond between Afghan Hound and owner have survived the generations.

origin. A number of countries have made names for themselves by producing top-quality Afghan Hounds. Interestingly, there is a certain look or type that many people associate with certain countries, although undoubtedly this is brought about, in part, by seeing images of individual influential dogs.

THE AFGHAN HOUND IN THE UNITED STATES

Miss Manson travelled to America in the mid-1920s and was to spread the following of Afghan Hounds to this part of the world. There was also importation of the Ghazni breeding to America. By the 1950s, such famous names as Mrs Sunny Shay with her Grandeurs and Mrs Kay Finch of the Crown Crest kennel were established top-winning and highly influential Afghan Hound breeders. The major winner, Ch Crown Crest Mr Universe, remains an all-time famous Afghan Hound in American dog-showing history. In 1957 Ch Shirkhan of Grandeur won Best in Show at the Westminster Kennel Club show, America's top dog show. Many later kennels have made huge and enduring names for themselves as producers of many top-quality and highly influential dogs; these include Akaba, Mecca, Stormhill, Coastwind, Kabik and many others.

THE AFGHAN HOUND AROUND THE WORLD

Miss Manson also sent one of her Bell-Murray-influenced hounds,

Begum of Cove, to the Netherlands to form the foundation of the Barukhzy kennels of Mrs Jungeling. The Oranje Manege kennels of Miss Eva Paupit remains one of the most famous names in Afghans, not only in the Netherlands but around the world as well.

Much of the original breeding in Germany was based on the Oranje Manege, or vdOM, breeding. The Scandinavian Afghan Hounds are also world famous, with the El Khyrias kennel of Christina Jernberg producing many, many top dogs for Sweden. The influential Tuohi Tikan kennel, of Anna-Leena and Pirkko Konttinen of Finland; the

Boxadan kennel, of Hanne and Finn Lassen of Denmark, and latterly, of Lotte and Ulf Jorgensen, also of Denmark, were all instrumental in forming the foundation of the present-day dogs in the Scandinavian countries. Other kennels have also contributed greatly to the success of the Scandinavian Afghan Hounds.

Australia initially obtained most of its imports through Britain, with some American influence. Carloway was one of the influential kennels to export stock to support early Australian breeding. Early kennels include Furbari, el Tazi, Fermoy, Calahorra and many others.

The author with four generations of her Afghans.

Opposite page, left: Cloudside Tropical Ginger of Kharisar is a typical, modern Afghan Hound.

During the 1970s, when their beauty, grace and hairstyling fitted in with the trends in fashion of the era, Afghan Hounds were subjected to a major population explosion. At this time the breed became excessively popular and was catapulted into the limelight in a most unsuitable manner for any breed. The result of popularity of this kind, with any type of dog, is that the breed is acquired for aspects that are appealing to the public *en masse* and many aspects of the breed are overlooked by prospective owners. The result for the Afghan Hound was that many people who purchased these dogs completely misunderstood them and the breed gained a reputation that was often unfair and untrue. It has distressed me, over the years, to hear the Afghan Hound labelled as a stupid and difficult breed, since the truth is that they are, in general, totally the opposite.

DID YOU KNOW?

Afghan Hounds have a reputation for running away when off the lead. I prefer to think of this as the dog obeying its natural instinct in the call of wild and open places rather than

naughtiness. However, it is still rather annoying. Don't expect to be able to teach your Afghan Hound to come back to you when it is running free, although it is always worth trying. It is better to work with this aspect of the breed than to fight it, so it is sensible to try to find safe, secure free running areas rather than to test your dog in open land.

PHYSICAL CHARACTERISTICS

Afghan Hounds are large, graceful, beautiful dogs. The body of this breed should be balanced and possess total soundness of construction. The chest should be relatively deep and well sprung to allow plenty of room for lungs and heart. The Afghan Hound should be a well-muscled dog, without coarseness, the whole dog

INFORMATION...

The Afghan Hound is unusual in being a breed where rather prominent hip bones are required by the Kennel Club standard. These bones should be seen and felt, despite the

dog's being of satisfactory weight and in good body condition. The bones referred to are those at either side of the dog's spine a few inches above the root of the tail. These relatively prominent bones are the start of a correct croup formation, which is so important in the tail carriage and in the whole action and construction of the dog.

being built for speed and power. This breed should be capable of tremendous strength and turn of speed when running. The graceful, balanced movement is a great feature of the breed. The Kennel Club standard describes the movement as having a 'style of high order' and this describes the way the Afghan moves extremely well. The typical Afghan Hound moves with a unique light and yet strong, springy yet true step. With its tail and head raised, the moving Afghan Hound draws the eye totally. As with any hunting breed, soundness of movement is essential to enable the dog to function within its original skills.

The head of the Afghan Hound is a very interesting feature of the breed, since Afghan

Female Afghan Hounds showing the typical short-coated face.

This is the bone at the back of the skull, which is less noticeable in many other breeds.

A unique feature of the breed is the coat pattern. This is most amazing to those who have not seen a typical coat pattern in an Afghan Hound before. The coat on the face, sides of the neck and saddle (a saddle-shaped area on the back, elongated to include the whole of the spine from the nape of the neck to the root of the tail) is short and close. There may also be areas of short coat (which may be under the silky long coat and not seen unless exposed by lifting the longer coat) on the pasterns, the wrists of a dog. Since these areas of short coat are combined with long, silky fine coat over the rest of the body, the whole dog is quite remarkable to look at. There are variations in coat pattern, some Afghan Hounds will never gain a saddle, even when fully adult, some will only have a saddle after coat-loss periods. Some will lose an excessive amount of the silky coat, carrying only a sparse sprinkling of this coat type and far more areas of short, saddle-type coat than is generally seen. This type of coat

Hounds are short coated on the face, all the expression is clearly visible. The bone structure is, or should be, very beautiful, with the different planes and bone lines giving an effect of the head having been chiselled. Coupled with this and largely because of the bones around the eyes, the eyes should be almost triangular in shape, with the inner to outer, lower edge slanting somewhat upwards to achieve this shaping. The eyes are often relatively deeply set, adding to the expression. The true Afghan Hound expression of aloof disdain and the impression described in the standard of 'looking at and through' one are yet more additions to the individuality of the breed. The head also has another distinctive requirement, that of a prominent occiput.

DID YOU KNOW?

When an Afghan Hound moults, the coat forms mats, so always expect extra work with the brush at this time.

pattern, more common before the 1960s and '70s, was generally referred to as the Bell-Murray coat pattern.

One of the fascinating sides to the breed is the variation in colours that occur. Probably, in Britain, gold cream, with or without a black or shaded mask (face), and black, with gold, tan or silver markings (on the face, pasterns and tail root, for instance), are the more prevalent colours. However, all colours are accepted by the breed standard and some of these change throughout the dog's life in a fascinating way. For instance, a silver brindle Afghan Hound as a puppy may change to a dark grizzle colour in old age. To add additional interest to that of the actual colour, very often there will be a variation of type (a term often, perhaps erroneously, used to describe the various nuances in

DID YOU KNOW?

Afghan Hounds appear to have remarkably long memories. Afghan Hounds often seem to recognise their breeders with affection despite a long absence from their birth home. Afghan Hound dams also often appear to retain extremely strong ties with their offspring and frequently seem to recognise their grown puppies when they meet them.

head shape and expression, or familial variations, for instance), which typifies the different colours. One of the interesting colours is the domino, which gives the dog a reverse colouring to the black-masked dog. Domino Afghans have pale colouring on their faces and darker colouring on the body, often with a 'widow's peak' (a cap-like area over the skull) descending onto the forehead in a point.

Possibly one of the most distinctive features of the breed is

Although Afghan Hounds are aloof and independent-minded, they can be trustworthy and responsive to children.

Afghan Hounds are not always recommended for homes with children, but they do get along well with children who know how to treat a dog respectfully.

The ring on the dog's tail is a unique breed characteristic since it varies from dog to dog.

the typical ringed tail. This is most beautiful in the correct form. One of the aspects that determines the tail carriage is the distinctive hip placement of the Afghan Hound. The typically prominent hip bones are quite an unusual constructional requirement. From these hip bones there is a slope of the croup, to the root of the tail. The tail is then held at a raised angle when the dog is aroused or moving, or down in repose with, in its typical form, a full ring on the end. This is a most unusual requirement for a dog and is another of the unique aspects that distinguishes the Afghan Hound. There is a variation of degree of ring on the tail of Afghan Hounds; some possess only a sickle shape towards the end of the tail. Often the ring of the tail is not fully developed until after the puppy

has completed teething; sometimes it is visible from early puppyhood.

I am sure that, when first seen by Europeans, the Afghan Hounds of Afghanistan created a huge degree of interest, as they possess so many unique and unusual features. This is a breed of enormous individuality. Nowadays, since the breed has undergone such a degree of exposure, most people are used to the appearance of these dogs, but consider the stir they must have made when they were first exported from Afghanistan. Add their reputation of character, and they must have attracted a fascinated following wherever they went.

PERSONALITY

It is necessary to understand the Afghan Hound character to appreciate it fully. For many, the idiosyncrasies of this breed make it virtually impossible to live without, to others the breed is

nearly impossible to live with. One of the aspects that determine this outcome is your house, another is your garden or grounds around your home but the main aspect is your own personality and that of the rest of your family.

The typical Afghan Hound is very much a creature of independent thought and free spirit. The easiest way to live with this is to simply accept it. However, the breed is also loving. Afghan Hounds are capable of as much love and devotion as anyone could possibly crave, but this love is not always given in a demonstrative way; it is often given at a distance.

I believe that the Afghan Hound is one of the most intelligent breeds I have ever lived with, but the intelligence is not shown in learning to do tricks or in any form of training. Afghan Hounds are self-taught, meaning that they

DID YOU KNOW?

The feet of the Afghan Hound should be large with well-arched toes and may look quite ungainly in the baby

puppy. Large feet are better able to cover the original ground on which Afghan Hounds lived in their native Afghanistan.

generally do not copy the behaviour of other dogs; instead, they create their own. It could be unwise to try to bend the will of a true Afghan Hound to your path; rather, it is necessary to travel a path parallel to your Afghan Hound. I have often spent time sitting on the floor whilst our Afghan Hounds occupied the sofa.

Who can resist a face like this? Although not the breed for everyone, the Afghan's personality is like no other in dogdom and has won the breed its share of devout admirers.

I realise that this is uncomfortable, but I have accepted that this is part of the breed and that (in the dogs' minds) we are equals. Sometimes, I have resisted the looks of indignation and reproach and insisted on having a place in comfort myself.

It is not really sensible to acquire an Afghan Hound if you wish to have a dog that you can 'master.' Although you should not be mastered by your Afghan Hound either, you can expect to have an equal in your family when you have an Afghan Hound in it. Typical Afghan Hounds are not subservient to anyone and will sometimes show passing aggression if they are pushed to prove this.

Although, as individuals, many Afghan Hounds are excellent and trustworthy with children, this is not a breed that one could really recommend as a dog universally suitable for them. This is mainly because Afghan Hounds do not suffer teasing well, as a rule. Obviously no dog should be subjected to teasing, but many breeds will overlook innocent, childish, irritating behaviour that an Afghan Hound would, perhaps, find relatively difficult to bear. Teasing of a dog with the sensitive personality of many Afghan Hounds could result in the dog's becoming withdrawn and anxious around children. In some instances, this might even lead to aggression, due to the anxiety and stress caused to the dog. This is not to say that all Afghan Hounds are the same, and I have seen adult males lying under toddlers as the toddlers have climbed on top of them, with no hint of concern or unpleasantness from the dogs! With any dog, it is necessary to supervise young children at all times.

One of the truest and, indeed, unique characteristics is the expression, which, as described in the Kennel Club standard, looks 'at and through' one. This, I feel, is saved by Afghan Hounds for studying the horizon and surveying strangers and minor acquaintances. I find that the privileged inner circle of the Afghan Hounds' closest and dearest people is often accorded a loving and intimate gaze. There can be nothing more rewarding to an Afghan Hound lover than this gaze—it is confidential, it is personal and it speaks totally from the heart. It is possible, when you really know your dog, to communicate in total silence. On the subject of communication, I believe that the Afghan Hound is able to acquire one of the largest understandings of human vocabulary of any of the breeds that I have lived with. However, words such as 'come,' 'stay' and 'no' are often carefully considered first, before an acceptance can be negotiated.

All of this independence makes the Afghan Hound more of a specialist breed than a typical 'pet' breed. This does not mean that Afghans do not make good companions to the non-exhibiting owner, it just means that they are not, necessarily, the sort of dog to fit into all households. In this discussion of Afghan Hound temperament, I have described the temperament that has typified the breed for generations. It could be argued that, in recent years, the trend has been towards a somewhat easier temperament in some ways, due to selective breeding. Many Afghan Hounds

These magnificent bitches clearly portray the majestic dignity that is a defining trait of the breed.

DID YOU KNOW?

The correct coat pattern of the Afghan Hound is most unusual. The short, dense, coarser hair of the saddle should continue along the whole length of the back, descending further down the sides of the dog just behind the shoulders to form a saddle-like shape. This short coat may also be seen on the pasterns of the dog and sometimes on the front of the backlegs, between the hock joint level and the foot. Often this saddle coat is seasonal and will appear only after times of coat moults. For some Afghan Hounds, the coat patterning is never achieved naturally in any form.

An Afghan cannot be definitively checked for hip dysplasia until it is two years of age.

nowadays are more outgoing to strangers, bouncier and nearer to other, less aloof breeds. Whether this is a satisfactory trend is a point for debate; many who know the Afghan Hound temperament in all its glory would vehemently defend the original traits as superior. I, personally, would prefer not to be greeted as a long-lost friend by an Afghan Hound who does not know me, but I can see that it is easier to walk in public places with this type of dog than with a reserved, shy and sometimes anxious dog.

To appreciate these dogs, it is essential to understand them. It is necessary to think like an Afghan Hound to see the world through the dog's eyes. Afghan Hounds I have lived with have borne strong links to their historical origins, they have held strong opinions of their own self-worth and they have expected a high degree of comfort and respect around their home. I do not believe that Afghan Hounds function well as kennel dogs, as these hounds require the proximity of like-minded humans to make undemanding and relaxed companions. These are not lap-dogs, they are deeply committed friends.

BREED-SPECIFIC HEALTH CONSIDERATIONS

Afghan Hounds are fortunate in having a reputation for being prone to very few of the more well-known canine inherited problems. There are, however, some conditions that the would-be owner may wish to know more about.

HIP DYSPLASIA

Hip dysplasia is a distressing condition that affects the hip joint. The hip is a ball-and-socket joint that may be affected by, mainly, the socket's not being deep enough or being incorrectly formed. When this occurs, a general laxity of the hip results. Often, the consequences are changes of an arthritic nature that take place in the joint. This condition is a painful one, and the dog suffers lameness and pain if arthritis is present.

Potential breeding stock can be x-rayed for signs of this condition and a number of breeders will take the opportunity of having their dogs routinely x-rayed. A veterinary surgeon takes the x-rays, often with the dog under anaesthetic. Following this, the x-rays are sent, in Britain, to the British Veterinary Association (BVA)/Kennel Club scheme and examined. Two veterinary surgeons from a panel check the x-rays against a specified formula. The scoring system used gives breeders the opportunity to ascertain the severity of the dog's hip conditions. There are variations from country to country

DID YOU KNOW?

The close coat on the face of an Afghan Hound allows the easy viewing of these dogs' wonderful expressions.

However, many young Afghan Hounds, of say 5–15 months, carry a lot of soft coat on the face that is termed puppy or monkey whiskers. Sometimes a puppy has so much of this coat that it is hard to imagine the beautiful refined head beneath. This coat should be lost naturally at the time of the first big coat change.

of scoring methods and regulations regarding breeding from affected dogs. In Britain the minimum score for each hip is zero and the maximum score, or most seriously affected, is 53. There are not high numbers of Afghan Hounds that have had x-rays submitted to the BVA/KC scheme by their owners. Consequently, it is not really possible to say to what level the Afghan Hound as a breed is affected by this condition.

EYE PROBLEMS

Cataracts: There are two types of cataract to be discussed here. There is a cataract that causes an opacity of the lens of one or both eyes, appears in the older Afghan Hound, is not considered hereditary and may affect any breed.

During the 1970s, however, there was much concern regarding young Afghan Hounds with cataracts. These were found to be passed on through families, i.e. inherited. Much work was undertaken to eradicate dogs carrying this defect from breeding programmes.

Entropion: Entropion is a term used to describe inversion of the eyelid and eyelashes. This causes irritation to the eyes, and may result in eye infection and weeping. The condition is generally considered to be inherited and is thought by some experts to be brought about by the repeated selection of dogs with small eyes (whatever the breed) for breeding. Entropion can be treated by a relatively simple operation. However, dogs affected with this defect should not be used for breeding, even if it has been surgically corrected.

MOUTH PROBLEMS

In Afghan Hounds the upper incisors should fit closely over the lower incisors, touching yet overlapping them in a scissor bite. It is acceptable, but not ideal, for the upper and lower incisors to meet together exactly, a bite known as level. Although this is permitted, it is a bite that is prone to alteration by becoming undershot (the lower incisors to protrude) with age. In addition, a level bite will often cause increased wearing of the incisors.

In some dogs, individual or groups of the lower incisors may protrude out of line, thus overlapping the corresponding upper incisors. This type of mouth is termed a 'wry mouth.' The mouth is uneven and may be less efficient to a hunting dog. This type of mouth is unlikely to seriously affect most dogs kept as companions. However, with a wry mouth, an Afghan is not suitable for showing. Since mouth defects are often passed on to future generations, it would be unwise to breed from an Afghan Hound with a wry mouth.

DO YOU KNOW ABOUT HIP DYSPLASIA?

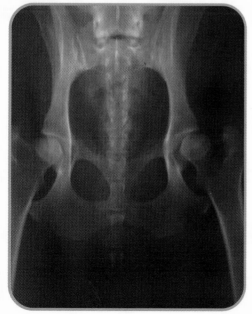

X-ray of a dog with 'Good' hips.

X-ray of a dog with 'Moderate' dysplastic hips.

Hip dysplasia is a fairly common condition found in purebred dogs. When a dog has hip dysplasia, its hind leg has an incorrectly formed hip joint. By constant use of the hip joint, it becomes more and more loose, wears abnormally and may become arthritic.

Hip dysplasia can only be confirmed with an x-ray, but certain symptoms may indicate a problem. Your dog may have a hip dysplasia problem if it walks in a peculiar manner, hops instead of smoothly runs, uses his hind legs in unison (to keep the pressure off the weak joint), has trouble getting up from a prone position or always sits with both legs together on one side of its body.

As the dog matures, it may adapt well to life with a bad hip, but in a few years the arthritis develops and many dogs with hip dysplasia become cripples.

Hip dysplasia is considered an inherited disease and only can be diagnosed definitively when the dog is two years old. Some experts claim that a special diet might help your puppy outgrow the bad hip, but the usual treatments are surgical. The removal of the pectineus muscle, the removal of the round part of the femur, reconstructing the pelvis and replacing the hip with an artificial one are all surgical interventions that are expensive, but they are usually very successful. Follow the advice of your veterinary surgeon.

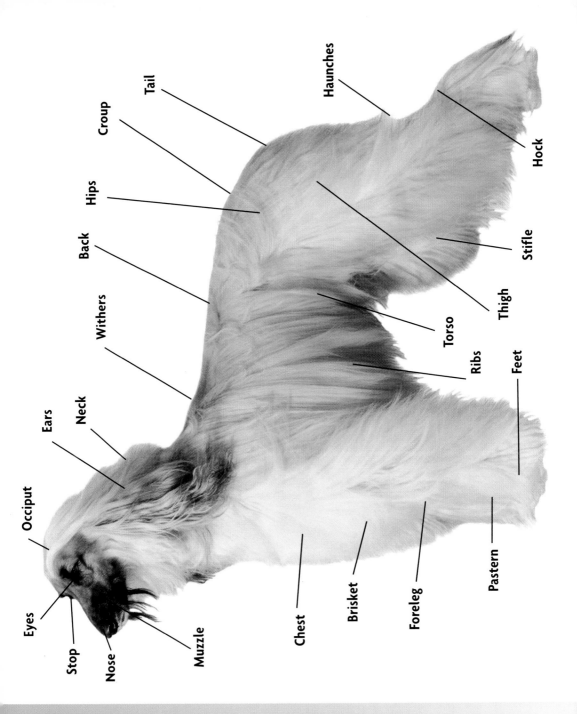

Physical Structure of the Afghan Hound

THE BREED STANDARD FOR THE
AFGHAN HOUND

In any breed, the standard is the description of the ideal dog of that breed. All typical specimens of the Afghan Hound will have many attributes that are described in the standard. From a show viewpoint, those Afghan Hounds that are considered the very best of their breed will be those that conform most closely to all aspects of the standard.

However, the standard has to be interpreted by each individual and, although in many respects the majority may agree, there will always be

A typical, high-quality Afghan Hound that measures well against the breed standard.

Correct head.

Incorrect head, snipey and with too much stop.

Incorrect head with too much resemblance to that of a Borzoi.

variations and arguments on the finer points amongst breeders, exhibitors and judges. This is not to suggest unfair bias but to acknowledge the right to freedom of choice. For instance, some judges will see a correctly ringed tail as being more essential to the Afghan Hound to render it typical of the breed, and others would place more emphasis on the correctly shaped eye as giving the desired typical expression. Both are important within the judging ring but, if a judge is faced with two dogs otherwise equal, a choice has to be made between them and these may, hypothetically, be the points that separate them.

In countries outside Britain, there are variations to the Kennel Club's standard. These variations must be taken into account when judges are officiating outside their own country.

Regardless of individual variations in interpreting the standard, experienced and knowledgeable judges have no difficulty in using the standard to obtain a blueprint by which they judge the breed.

THE KENNEL CLUB STANDARD FOR THE AFGHAN HOUND
General Appearance: Gives the impression of strength and dignity, combining speed and power. Head held proudly.

Characteristics: Eastern or Oriental expression is typical of breed. The Afghan looks at and through one.

Temperament: Dignified and aloof, with a certain keen fierceness.

Head and Skull: Skull long, not too narrow, with prominent occiput. Foreface long with punishing jaws and slight stop. Skull well balanced and mounted by a long 'top-knot.'

Eyes: Dark for preference, but golden colour not debarred. Nearly triangular, slanting slightly upwards from inner corner to outer corner.

Ears: Set low and well back, carried close to head. Covered with long silky hair.

Mouth: Jaws strong, with a perfect, regular and complete scissor bite, i.e. upper teeth closely overlapping lower teeth and set square to the jaws. Level bite tolerated.

Neck: Long, strong, with proud carriage of head.

Forequarters: Shoulders long and sloping, well set back, well muscled and strong without being loaded. Forelegs straight and well boned, straight with shoulder,

Weak front, turning out.

Correct forequarters; straight legs in line with shoulder.

elbows close to ribcage, turning neither in nor out.

Body: Back level, moderate length, well muscled, back falling slightly away to stern. Loin straight, broad and rather short. Hipbones rather prominent and wide apart. A fair spring of ribs and good depth of chest.

Hindquarters: Powerful, well bent and well turned stifles. Great length between hip and hock, with comparatively short distance between hock and foot. Dewclaws may be removed.

Incorrect 'tea-handle' tail.

Correct tail with ring at end.

Rear too high; over-angulated stifle.

Correct level back.

A show trot in 2-time, confident and graceful.

Bad gait; pacing.

Feet: Forefeet strong and very large both in length and breadth, and covered with long thick hair; toes arched. Pasterns long and springy, pads well down on ground. Hindfeet long, but not quite as broad as forefeet; covered with long thick hair.

Tail: Not too short. Set on low with ring at end. Raised when in action. Sparsely feathered.

Gait/Movement: Smooth and springy with a style of high order.

Coat: Long and very fine texture on ribs, fore and hindquarters and flanks. In mature dogs from shoulder backwards and along the saddle, hair short and close. Hair long from forehead backwards, with a distinct silky 'top-knot.' On foreface hair short. Ears and legs well coated. Pasterns can be bare. Coat must develop naturally.

Colour: All colours acceptable.

Size: Ideal height: dogs 68–74 cms (27–29 ins), bitches: 63–69 cms (25–27 ins).

Faults: Any departure from the foregoing points should be considered a fault and the seriousness with which the fault should be regarded should be in exact proportion to its degree.

Note: Male animals should have two apparently normal testicles fully descended into the scrotum.

The strong jaws must support a perfect, regular scissor bite.

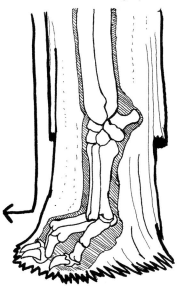

Frontal head study.

A correct foot; pastern springy but not weak.

An incorrect foot with straight pastern.

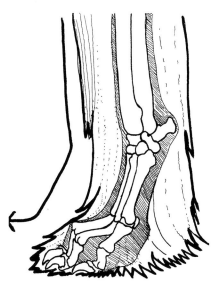

AFGHAN HOUND

A pup will be a pup! Be prepared for the mischief, antics and, of course, fun that comes with a new puppy.

that the dam must have been mismated by a Labrador. One of the reasons for this apparent disguise is the colouring of baby puppies. Even puppies that will eventually turn into palest cream gold in adulthood can be born almost black in appearance. One way to determine the potential colour is to turn the coat back with one finger and the pale colouring will be found at the roots of the hairs. Another way to predict the future colour is to look at the colour of the coat under the base of the newborn puppy's tail. Black and tan puppies will also often look black all over, the tan markings on the face, forelegs and hindlegs will be found, again, at the roots of the hairs.

Newborn Afghan Hound puppies are remarkably dissimilar to the adult version. When first faced with a newborn puppy many people find it extremely hard to believe they are actually Afghan Hounds. In fact, when our veterinary surgeon came to check over our first litter of Afghan Hounds, he told my mother that he was sure

Another reason that the newborn Afghan Hound looks

DID YOU KNOW?

You should not even think about buying a puppy that looks sick, undernourished, overly frightened or nervous. Sometimes a timid puppy will warm up to you after a 30-minute 'let's-get-acquainted' session.

so strange to the inexperienced eye is the difference in head to the adult. The baby puppy has a foreface that is almost rounded in appearance at the muzzle, belying the long, refined head to come. Although the trained eye will see through this and experienced breeders will be able to determine their own preferences at an extremely early age, to the inexperienced eye a baby puppy head will, perhaps, look as if it belongs to a different breed.

The Afghan Hound puppy is born with a short coat and this will continue to look short for many weeks. This gives the young puppy rather a gangly look from around the age you may first go to see the litter until 12 to 20 weeks or more. As the puppy's legs elongate and the puppy goes through all sorts of ungainly phases, you may wonder at the chances of your young puppy ever maturing into the elegant Afghan Hound of your dreams. However, with coat growth and body maturity, a lot of 'gawky' youngsters have turned into elegant adults.

In picking your Afghan Hound puppy out of those available in the litter, you will need, in many instances, to heed the advice of the breeder. An experienced breeder will know better than you how the

DO YOUR HOMEWORK!

Unfortunately, when a puppy is bought by someone who does not take into consideration the time and attention that dog ownership requires, it is the puppy who suffers when he is either abandoned or placed in a shelter by a frustrated owner. So all of the 'homework' you do in preparation for your pup's arrival will benefit you both. The more informed you are, the more you will know what to expect and the better equipped you

will be to handle the ups and downs of raising a puppy. Hopefully, everyone in the household is willing to do his part in raising and caring for the pup. The anticipation of owning a dog often brings a lot of promises from excited family members: 'I will walk him every day,' 'I will feed him,' 'I will housebreak him,' etc., but these things take time and effort, and promises can easily be forgotten once the novelty of the new pet has worn off.

immediate background of the litter's pedigree as are available. This will give you more of an idea what to expect in your own puppy. For instance, if all of them have rather light, round eyes it is likely, but still not inevitable, that your puppy will follow this trend. Likewise, coats are generally familial, so if you hope for a heavy coat or, conversely, if you yearn for the earlier, lighter type of coat pattern, the coats of the ancestors will give you a good guide.

The Afghan Hound is a large, long-boned breed. Afghan Hounds require careful rearing and must have the best of puppy diets to ensure that they receive the required vitamin and mineral intake, in the correct balance. Do take advice from your breeder and veterinary surgeon to ensure that your puppy receives the correct diet.

WHERE TO BEGIN?
If you are convinced that the Afghan Hound is the ideal dog for you, it's time to learn about where to find a puppy and what to look for. Locating a litter of Afghan Hounds should not present a problem for the new owner. You should enquire about breeders in your area who enjoy a good reputation in the breed. You are looking for an

puppies are likely to mature. For instance, although many Afghan Hound puppies have no curl to the end of the tail as babies of eight to ten weeks, this often comes with age; after teething is a common time.

Generally the individual look of the mature dog will be familial, so do try to see as many of the dogs in the established breeder with outstanding dog ethics and a strong commitment to the breed. New owners should have as many questions as they have doubts. An established breeder is indeed the one to answer your four million questions and make you comfortable with your choice of the Afghan Hound. An established breeder will sell you a puppy at a fair price if, and only if, the breeder determines that you are a suitable, worthy owner of his/her dogs. An established breeder can be relied upon for advice, no matter what time of day or night. A reputable breeder will accept a puppy back, without questions, should you decide that this is not the right dog for you.

CHOOSING A BREEDER

When choosing a breeder, reputation is much more important than convenience of location. Do not be overly impressed by breeders who run brag advertisements in the presses about their stupendous champions and working lines. The real quality breeders are quiet and unassuming. You hear about them at the dog trials and shows, by word of mouth. You may be well advised to avoid the novice who lives only a couple miles away. The local novice breeder, trying so hard to

DID YOU KNOW?

Your puppy should have a well-fed appearance but not a distended abdomen, which may indicate worms or incorrect feeding, or both. The body should be firm, with a solid feel. The skin of the abdomen should be pale pink and clean, without signs of scratching or rash. Check the hind legs to make certain that dewclaws were removed, if any were present at birth.

get rid of that first litter of puppies, is more than accommodating and anxious to sell you one. That breeder will charge you as much as any established

39

DOCUMENTATION

Two important documents you will get from the breeder are the pup's pedigree and registration certificate. The breeder should register the litter and each pup with The Kennel Club, and it is necessary for you to have the paperwork if you plan on showing or breeding in the future.

Make sure you know the breeder's intentions on which type of registration he will obtain for the pup. There are limited registrations which may prohibit the dog from being shown, bred or from competing in non-conformation trials such as Working or Agility if the breeder feels that the pup is not of sufficient quality to do so. There is also a type of registration that will permit the dog in non-conformation competition only.

On the reverse side of the registration certificate, the new owner can find the transfer section which must be signed by the breeder.

midnight or eat the family cat!

Whilst health considerations in the Afghan Hound are not nearly as daunting as in some other breeds, socialisation is a breeder concern of immense importance. Since the Afghan Hound's temperament can vary from line to line, socialisation is the first and best way to encourage a proper, stable personality.

Choosing a breeder is an important first step in dog ownership. Fortunately, the majority of Afghan Hound breeders are devoted to the breed and its well-being. New owners should have little problem finding a reputable breeder who doesn't live on the other side of the country (or in a different country). The Kennel

breeder. The novice breeder isn't going to interrogate you and your family about your intentions with the puppy, the environment and training you can provide, etc. That breeder will be nowhere to be found when your poorly bred, badly adjusted four-pawed monster starts to growl and spit up at

INSURANCE

Many good breeders will offer you insurance with your new puppy, which is an excellent idea. The first few weeks of insurance will probably be covered free of charge or with only minimal cost, allowing you to take up the policy when this expires. If you own a pet dog, it is sensible to take out such a policy as veterinary fees can be high, although routine vaccinations and boosters are not covered. Look carefully at the many options open to you before deciding which suits you best.

Club is able to recommend breeders of quality Afghan Hounds, as can any local all-breed club or Afghan Hound club. Potential owners are encouraged to attend dog shows to see the Afghan Hounds in action, to meet the owners and handlers firsthand and to get an of idea what Afghan Hounds look like outside a photographer's lens. Provided you approach the handlers when they are not terribly busy with the dogs, most are more than willing to answer questions, recommend breeders and give advice.

Now that you have contacted and met a breeder or two and made your choice about which breeder is best suited to your needs, it's time to visit the litter. Keep in mind that many top breeders have waiting lists. Sometimes new owners have to wait as long as two years for a puppy. If you are really committed to the breeder whom you've selected, then you will wait (and hope for an early arrival!). If not, you may have to resort to your second or third choice breeder. Don't be too anxious, however. If the breeder doesn't have any waiting list, or any customers, there is probably a good reason. It's no different than visiting a pub with no clientele. The

INFORMATION...

Breeders rarely release puppies until they are eight to ten weeks of age. This is an acceptable age for most breeds of dog, excepting toy breeds, which are not released until

around 12 weeks, given their petite sizes. If a breeder has a puppy that is 12 weeks or more, it is likely well socialised and housetrained. Be sure that it is otherwise healthy before deciding to take it home.

better pubs and restaurants always have a waiting list—and it's usually worth the wait. Besides, isn't a puppy more important than a pint?

Since you are likely to be choosing an Afghan Hound as a pet dog and not a show dog, you simply should select a pup that is friendly and appealing. Afghan Hounds generally have large litters, averaging seven puppies, so selection is good once you have located a

desirable litter. While the basic structure of the breed has little variation, the temperament may present trouble in certain strains. Beware of the shy or overly aggressive puppy: be especially conscious of the nervous Afghan Hound pup. Don't let sentiment or emotion trap you into buying the runt of the litter.

The gender of your puppy is largely a matter of personal taste, although many prefer females, males may be more affectionate. The difference in size is noticeable but slight. Coloration is fairly overwhelming with this breed, and there are many lovely combinations from which to choose. Rely upon your breeders to predict the adult colour of your puppy.

Breeders commonly allow visitors to see the litter by around the fifth or sixth week, and puppies leave for their new homes between the eighth and tenth week. Breeders who permit their puppies to leave early are more interested in your pounds than their puppies' well-being. Puppies need to learn the rules of the trade from their dams, and most dams continue teaching the pups manners and dos and don'ts until around the eighth week. Breeders spend significant amounts of time with the

Afghan Hound toddlers so that they are able to interact with the 'other species', i.e. humans. Bonding with the Afghan pup is critical as this breed is naturally aloof to people. A well-bred, well-socialised Afghan Hound pup should welcome humans but will never be as outgoing as a spaniel or a Labrador.

Always check the bite of your selected puppy to be sure that it is correct. It is important to check the soundness of the bite. There can be a problem with wry mouths in some lines.

COMMITMENT OF OWNERSHIP

After considering all of these factors, you have most likely already made some very important decisions about selecting your puppy. You have chosen an Afghan Hound, which means that you have decided that this unique breed with its strong will and mind will fit into your family and lifestyle. If you have selected a breeder, you have gone a step further—you have done your research and found a respon-sible, conscientious person who breeds quality Afghan Hounds and who should be a reliable source of help as you and your puppy adjust to life together. If you have observed a litter in action, you have obtained a firsthand look at the dynamics

YOUR SCHEDULE...

If you lead an erratic, unpredictable life, with daily or weekly changes in your work requirements, consider

the problems of owning a puppy. The new puppy has to be fed regularly, socialised (loved, petted, handled, introduced to other people) and, most importantly, allowed to visit outdoors for toilet training. As the dog gets older, it can be more tolerant of deviations in its feeding and toilet relief.

of a puppy 'pack' and, thus, you should learn about each pup's individual personality—perhaps you have even found one that particularly appeals to you.

However, even if you have not yet found the Afghan Hound puppy of your dreams, observing pups will help you learn to recognise certain behaviour and to determine what a pup's behaviour indicates about his temperament. You will be able to pick out which pups are the leaders, which ones are less outgoing, which ones are confident, which ones are shy, playful, friendly, aggressive, etc. Equally as important, you will learn to recognise what a healthy pup should look and act like. All of these things will help you in your search, and when you find the Afghan Hound that was meant for you, you will know it!

ARE YOU A FIT OWNER?

If the breeder from whom you are buying a puppy asks you a lot of personal questions, do not be

insulted. Such a breeder wants to be sure that you will be a fit provider for his puppy.

Researching your breed, selecting a responsible breeder and observing as many pups as possible are all important steps on the way to dog ownership. It may seem like a lot of effort... and you have not even brought the pup home yet! Remember, though, you cannot be too careful when it comes to deciding on the type of dog you want and finding out about your prospective pup's background. Buying a puppy is not—or should not be—just another whimsical purchase. This is one instance in which you actually do get to choose your own family! You may be thinking that buying a puppy should be fun—it should not be so serious and so much work. Keep in mind that your puppy is not a cuddly stuffed toy or decorative lawn ornament, but a creature that will become a real member of your family. You will come to realise that whilst buying a puppy is a pleasurable and exciting endeavour, it is not something to be taken lightly. Relax...the fun will start when the pup comes home!

Always keep in mind that a puppy is nothing more than a baby in a furry disguise...a baby who is virtually helpless in a human world and who trusts his owner for fulfilment of his basic needs for survival. In addition to water and shelter, your pup needs care, protection, guidance and love. If you are not prepared to commit to this, then you are not prepared to own a dog.

Wait a minute, you say. How hard could this be? All of my neighbours own dogs and they seem to be doing just fine. Why should I have to worry about all of this? Well, you should not worry about it; in fact, you will probably find that once your Afghan Hound pup gets used to his new home, he will fall into his place in the family quite naturally. But it never hurts to emphasise the commitment of dog ownership. With some time and patience, it is really not too difficult to raise a curious and trusting Afghan Hound pup to be a well-adjusted and well-mannered adult dog—a dog that could be your most loyal friend.

PREPARING PUPPY'S PLACE IN YOUR HOME

Researching your breed and finding a breeder are only two aspects of the 'homework' you will have to do before taking your Afghan Hound puppy home. You will also have to prepare your home and family for the new addition. Much as you would prepare a nursery for a newborn baby, you will need to designate a place in your home that will be the puppy's own. How you prepare your

home will depend on how much freedom the dog will be allowed. Whatever you decide, you must ensure that he has a place that he can 'call his own.'

When you bring your new puppy into your home, you are bringing him into what will become his home as well. Obviously, you did not buy a puppy so that he could take over your house, but in order for a puppy to grow into a stable, well-adjusted dog, he has to feel comfortable in his surroundings. Remember, he is leaving the warmth and security of his mother and littermates, as

DID YOU KNOW?

Taking your dog from the breeder to your home in a car can be a very uncomfortable experience for both

of you. The puppy will have been taken from his warm, friendly, safe environment and brought into a strange new environment. An environment that moves! Be prepared for loose bowels, urination, crying, whining and even fear biting. With proper love and encouragement when you arrive home, the stress of the trip should quickly disappear.

well as the familiarity of the only place he has ever known, so it is important to make his transition as easy as possible. By preparing a place in your home for the puppy, you are making him feel as welcome as possible in a strange new place. It should not take him long to get used to it, but the sudden shock of being transplanted is somewhat traumatic for a young pup. Imagine how a small child would feel in the same situation—that is how your puppy must be feeling. It is up to you to reassure him and to let him know, 'Little chap, you are going to like it here!'

WHAT YOU SHOULD BUY

CRATE

You may wish to purchase a crate for your Afghan Hound puppy. Do remember that these dogs need and seek human companionship and that, although a suitable dog crate can be a very useful and satisfactory indoor sanctuary for your puppy, it should only be used for short periods. It would not be suitable to keep an Afghan Hound cooped up for any but brief periods of time in a crate. Besides, once past the chewing stage, the Afghan Hound is generally an easy and relaxed companion who makes little more demand around the house than a very comfortable sofa and peace and quiet in which to enjoy it!

To someone unfamiliar with the use of crates in dog training, it may seem like punishment to shut a dog in a crate, but this is not the case at all. Although all breeders do not advocate crate training, more and more breeders and trainers are recommending crates as preferred tools for show puppies as well as pet puppies. Crates are not cruel—crates have many humane and highly effective uses in dog care and training. For example, crate training is a very popular and very successful housebreaking method. A crate can keep your dog safe during travel; moreover, a crate provides your dog with a place of his own in your home. It serves as a 'doggie bedroom' of sorts—your Afghan Hound can curl up in his crate when he wants to sleep or when he just needs a break. Many dogs sleep in their crates overnight. When lined with soft bedding and with a favourite toy inside, a crate becomes a cosy pseudo-den for your dog. Like his ancestors, he too will seek out the comfort and retreat of a den—you just happen to be providing him with something a little more luxurious than his early ancestors enjoyed.

As far as purchasing a crate,

CRATE TRAINING TIP

During crate training, you should partition off the section of the crate in which the pup stays. If he is given too big an area, this will hinder your training efforts. Crate training is based on the fact that a dog does not like to soil his sleeping quarters, so it is ineffective to keep a pup in a crate that is so big that he can eliminate in one end and get far

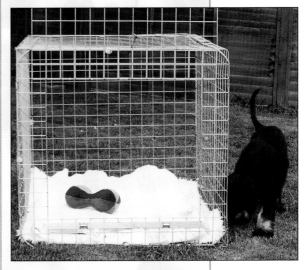

enough away from it to sleep. Also, you want to make the crate den-like for the pup. Blankets and a favourite toy will make the crate cosy for the small pup; as he grows, you may want to evict some of his 'roommates' to make more room.

It will take some coaxing at first, but be patient. Given some time to get used to it, your pup will adapt to his new home-within-a-home quite nicely.

Your local pet shop will have a variety of crates from which you can choose one that is suitable for your Afghan. Make certain that the crate you buy will accommodate your puppy when he is fully grown.

PHOTO COURTESY OF DOSKOCIL.

the type that you buy is up to you. It will most likely be one of the two most popular types: wire or fibreglass. There are advantages and disadvantages to each type. For example, a wire crate is more open, allowing the air to flow through and affording the dog a view of what is going on around him whilst a fibreglass crate is sturdier. Both can double as travel crates, providing protection for the dog. The size of the crate is another thing to consider.

Puppies do not stay puppies forever—in fact, sometimes it seems as if they grow right before your eyes. A small-sized crate may be fine for a very young Afghan Hound pup, but it will not do him much good for long! Unless you have the money and the inclination to buy a new crate every time your pup has a growth spurt, it is better to get one that will accommodate your dog both as a pup and at full size. A large-sized crate will be necessary for a full-grown Afghan Hound, who stands approximately 25–29 inches high.

BEDDING
Veterinary bedding in the dog's crate will help the dog feel more at home and you may also like to pop in a small blanket. This will take the place of the leaves, twigs, etc., that the pup would use in the wild to make a den; the pup can make his own 'burrow' in the crate. Although your pup is far removed from his den-making ancestors, the denning instinct is still a part of his genetic makeup. Second, until you bring your pup home, he has been sleeping amidst the warmth of his mother and litter-mates, and whilst a blanket is not the same as a warm, breathing body, it still provides heat and something with which to snuggle. You will want to

A wire crate is good for outdoor use as it allows a better flow of air and affords the dog an unobstructed view of his surroundings. Always place the crate in an area that provides adequate shade.

Before your pup's arrival to your home, purchase a good sized bed and some safe, chew toys.

NATURAL TOXINS

Examine your grass and garden landscaping before bringing your puppy home. Many varieties of plants have leaves, stems or flowers that are toxic if ingested, and you can

depend on a curious puppy to investigate them. Ask your vet for information on poisonous plants or research them at your library.

dog will enjoy playing with his favourite toys, whilst you will enjoy the fact that they distract him from your expensive shoes and leather sofa. Puppies love to chew; in fact, chewing is a physical need for pups as they are teething, and everything looks appetising! The full range of your possessions—from old tea towel to Oriental carpet—are fair game in the eyes of a teething pup. Puppies are not all that discerning when it comes to finding something to literally 'sink their teeth into'—everything tastes great!

Afghan Hound puppies are fairly aggressive chewers and only the hardest, strongest toys should be offered to them. Breeders advise owners to resist stuffed toys, because they can

Rope toys should be used with discretion as tugging games may over-stimulate an Afghan Hound.

wash your pup's bedding frequently in case he has an accident in his crate, and replace or remove any blanket that becomes ragged and starts to fall apart.

Toys

Toys are a must for dogs of all ages, especially for curious playful pups. Puppies are the 'children' of the dog world, and what child does not love toys? Chew toys provide enjoyment for both dog and owner—your

Puppies should always have toys available for chewing. Simply put, dogs must chew. Be sure the toys you provide are safe.

become de-stuffed in no time. The overly excited pup may ingest the stuffing, which is neither digestible nor nutritious.

Similarly, squeaky toys are quite popular, but must be avoided for the Afghan Hound. Perhaps a squeaky toy can be used as an aid in training, but not for free play. If a pup 'disembowels' one of these, the small plastic squeaker inside can be dangerous if swallowed. Monitor the condition of all your pup's toys carefully and get rid of any that have been chewed to the point of becoming potentially dangerous.

Be careful of natural bones, which have a tendency to splinter into sharp, dangerous pieces. Also be careful of rawhide, which can turn into pieces that are easy to swallow or into a mushy mess on your carpet.

Natural bones are not recommended for puppies since they usually can be broken into sharp pieces and ingested.

TOYS, TOYS, TOYS!

With a big variety of dog toys available, and so many that look like they would be a lot of fun for a dog, be careful in your selection. It is amazing what a set of puppy teeth can do to an innocent-

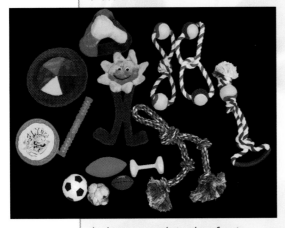

looking toy, so, obviously, safety is a major consideration. Be sure to choose the most durable products that you can find. Hard nylon bones and toys are a safe bet, and many of them are offered in different scents and flavours that will be sure to capture your dog's attention. It is always fun to play a game of catch with your dog, and there are balls and flying discs that are specially made to withstand dog teeth.

LEAD

A nylon lead is probably the best option as it is the most resistant to puppy teeth should your pup take a liking to chewing on his lead. Of course, this is a habit that should be nipped in the bud, but if your pup likes to chew on his lead he has a very slim chance of being able to chew through the strong nylon. Nylon leads are also lightweight, which is good for a young Afghan Hound who is just getting used to the idea of walking on a lead. For everyday walking and safety purposes, the nylon lead is a good choice. As your pup grows up and gets used to walking on the lead, you may want to purchase a flexible lead. These leads allow you to extend the length to give the dog a broader area to explore or to shorten the length to keep the dog close to you. Of course there are special leads for training purposes, and specially made leather harnesses for adventurous

Your local pet shop should be able to help you with the selection of your Afghan's lead. Leads come in various sizes, colours and prices.

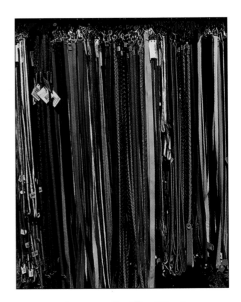

Afghan Hounds, but these are not necessary for routine walks.

COLLAR

Your pup should get used to wearing a collar all the time since you will want to attach his ID tags to it and you have to attach the lead to something! A lightweight nylon collar is a good choice; make sure that it fits snugly enough so that the pup cannot wriggle out of it, but is loose enough so that it will not be uncomfortably tight around the pup's neck. You should be able to fit a finger between the pup and the collar. It may take some time for your pup to get used to wearing the collar, but soon he will not even notice that it is there. Choke

The Afghan's long coat can be protected with garments made especially for that purpose.

collars are made for training, but should only be used by an experienced handler.

FOOD AND WATER BOWLS

Your pup will need two bowls, one for food and one for water. You may want two sets of bowls, one for inside and one for outside, depending on where the dog will be fed and where he will be spending most of his time. Stainless steel or sturdy plastic bowls are popular choices. Plastic bowls are more chewable. Dogs tend not to chew on the steel variety, which can be sterilised. It is important to buy sturdy bowls since anything is in danger of being chewed by puppy teeth and you do not want your dog to be

RESPONSIBILITY

Grooming tools, collars, leashes, dog beds and, of course, toys will be an expense to you when you first obtain your pup, and the cost will continue throughout your dog's lifetime. If your puppy damages or destroys your possessions (as most puppies surely will!) or something belonging to a neighbour, you can calculate additional expense. There is also flea and pest control, which every dog owner faces more than once. You must be able to handle the financial responsibility of owning a dog.

The **BUCKLE COLLAR** is the standard collar used for everyday purpose. Be sure that you adjust the buckle on growing puppies. Check it every day. It can become too tight overnight! These collars can be made of leather or nylon. Attach your dog's identification tags to this collar.

The **CHOKE COLLAR** is the usual collar recommended for training. It is constructed of highly polished steel so that it slides easily through the stainless steel loop. The idea is that the dog controls the pressure around its neck and he will stop pulling if the collar becomes uncomfortable. Never leave a choke collar on your dog when not training.

The **HALTER** is for a trained dog that has to be restrained to prevent running away, chasing a cat and the like. Considered the most humane of all collars, it is frequently used on smaller dogs for which collars are not comfortable.

constantly chewing apart his bowl (for his safety and for your purse!).

CLEANING SUPPLIES

Until a pup is housetrained you will be doing a lot of cleaning. Accidents will occur, which is okay in the beginning because the puppy does not know any better. All you can do is be prepared to clean up any 'accidents.' Old rags, towels, newspapers and a safe disinfectant are good to have on hand.

BEYOND THE BASICS

The items previously discussed are the bare necessities. You

Your local pet shop will have an assortment of dog bowls from which you can make a selection according to size, colour and price.

You should clean up after your dog, even if it is in your own garden. Your local pet shop should help you with devices, which make the task simpler.

Photo courtesy of Mikki Pet Products.

55

DID YOU KNOW?

Some experts in canine health advise that stress during a dog's early years of development can compromise

and weaken his immune system and may trigger the potential for a shortened life expectancy. They emphasise the need for happy and stress-free growing-up years.

will find out what else you need as you go along—grooming supplies, flea/tick protection, baby gates to partition a room, etc. These things will vary depending on your situation but it is important that you have everything you need to feed and make your Afghan Hound comfortable in his first few days at home.

PUPPY-PROOFING YOUR HOME

Aside from making sure that your Afghan Hound will be comfortable in your home, you also have to make sure that your home is safe for your Afghan Hound. This means taking precautions that your pup will not get into anything he should avoid and that there is nothing

DID YOU KNOW?

It will take at least two weeks for your puppy to become accustomed to his new surroundings. Give him

lots of love, attention, handling, frequent opportunities to relieve himself, a diet he likes to eat and a place he can call his own.

within his reach that may harm him should he sniff it, chew it, inspect it, etc. This probably seems obvious since, whilst you are primarily concerned with your pup's safety, at the same time you do not want your belongings to be ruined. Breakables should be placed out of reach if your dog is to have full run of the house. If he is to be limited to certain places within the house, keep any potentially dangerous items in the 'off-limits' areas. An electrical cord can pose a danger should the puppy decide to taste it—and who is going to convince a pup that it would not make a great chew toy? Cords should be fastened tightly against the wall. If your dog is going to spend time in a crate, make sure that there is nothing near his crate that he can reach if he sticks his curious little nose or paws through the openings. Just as you would with a child, keep all household cleaners and chemicals where the pup cannot reach them.

It is also important to make certain that the outside of your home is safe. Of course your puppy should never be unsupervised, but a pup let loose in the garden will want to run and explore, and he should

Be sure that your Afghan doesn't raid the dustbin. It might contain something harmful to the dog's health!

Afghans are athletic dogs. They can jump fairly high, so the fence must be of adequate height to keep your dog securely in the garden.

be granted that freedom. Do not let a fence give you a false sense of security; you would be surprised how crafty (and persistent) a dog can be in working out how to dig under and squeeze his way through small holes, or to jump or climb over a fence. The remedy is to make the fence high enough so that it really is impossible for your dog to get over it (about 3 metres should suffice), and well-embedded into the ground. Be sure to repair or secure any gaps in the fence. Check the fence periodically to ensure that it is in good shape and make repairs as needed; a very determined pup may return to the same spot to 'work on it' until he is able to get through.

FIRST TRIP TO THE VET

You have picked out your puppy, and your home and family are ready. Now all you have to do is collect your Afghan Hound from the breeder and the fun begins, right? Well…not so fast. Something else you need to prepare is your pup's first trip to the veterinary surgeon. Perhaps the breeder can recommend someone in the area that specialises in Afghan Hounds, or maybe you know some other Afghan Hound owners who can suggest a good vet. Either way, you should have an appointment arranged for your pup before you pick him up and plan on taking him for an examination before bringing him home.

The pup's first visit will consist of an overall examination to make sure that the pup does not have any problems that are not apparent to the eye. The veterinary surgeon will also set up a schedule for the pup's

BOY OR GIRL?

An important consideration to be discussed is the sex of your puppy. For a family companion, a bitch may be the better choice, considering the female's inbred concern for all young creatures and her accompanying tolerance and patience. It is always advisable to spay a pet bitch, which may guarantee her a longer life.

vaccinations; the breeder will inform you of which ones the pup has already received and the vet can continue from there.

INTRODUCTION TO THE FAMILY

Everyone in the house will be excited about the puppy coming home and will want to pet him and play with him, but it is best to make the introduction low-key so as not to overwhelm the puppy. He is apprehensive already. It is the first time he has been separated from his mother and the breeder, and the ride to your home is likely to be the first time he has been in a car. The last thing you want to do is smother him, as this is the wrong approach for an Afghan. This is not to say that human contact is not extremely necessary at this stage, because this is the time when a connection between the pup and his human family is formed. Gentle petting and soothing words should help console him, as well as just putting him down and letting him explore on his own (under your watchful eye, of course).

The pup may approach the family members or may busy himself with exploring for a while. Gradually, each person should spend some time with the pup, one at a time, crouching down to get as close

PUPPY PERSONALITY

When a litter becomes available to you, choosing a pup out of all those adorable faces will not be an easy task! Sound temperament is of utmost importance, but each pup has its own personality and some may be better suited to you than others. A feisty, independent pup will do well in a home with older children and adults, whilst quiet, shy puppies will thrive in a home with minimum noise and distractions. Your breeder knows the pups best and should be able to guide you in the right direction.

to the pup's level as possible and letting him sniff each person's hands and petting him gently. He definitely needs human attention and he needs

Introduce yourself to the pup by crouching to his level and letting him sniff your hand to get acquainted.

to be touched—this is how to form an immediate bond. Just remember that the pup is experiencing a lot of things for the first time, at the same time. There are new people, new noises, new smells and new things to investigate, so be gentle, be affectionate and be as comforting as you can be.

**YOUR PUP'S
FIRST NIGHT HOME**
You have travelled home with your new charge safely in his crate. He's been to the vet for a thorough check-up; he's been weighed, his papers examined; perhaps he's even been vaccinated and wormed as well. He's met the family, including the excited children and the less-than-happy cat. He's explored his area, his new bed, the garden and anywhere else he's been permitted. He's eaten his first meal at home and relieved himself in the proper place. He's heard lots of new sounds, smelled new friends and seen more of the outside world than ever before.

That was just the first day! He's worn out and is ready for bed...or so you think!

It's puppy's first night and you are ready to say 'Good night'—keep in mind that this is puppy's first night ever to be sleeping alone. His dam and littermates are no longer at paw's length and he's a bit scared, cold and lonely. Be reassuring to your new family member. However, this is not the time to spoil him and give in to his inevitable whining.

Puppies whine. They whine to let the others know where they are and hopefully to get company out of it. Place your pup in his new bed or crate in his room and close the door. Mercifully, he may fall asleep without a peep. When the inevitable occurs, ignore the whining; he is fine. Be strong and keep his interest in mind. Do not allow yourself to feel guilty and visit the pup. He will fall asleep.

Many breeders recommend placing a piece of bedding from his former home in his new bed so that he recognises the scent of his littermates. Others still advise placing a hot water bottle in his bed for warmth. This latter may be a good idea provided the pup doesn't attempt to suckle—he'll get good and wet and may not fall asleep so fast.

Puppy's first night can be somewhat stressful for the pup and his new family. Remember that you are setting the tone of nighttime at your house. Unless you want to play with your pup every evening at 10 p.m., midnight and 2 a.m., don't initiate the habit. Your family will thank you, and so will your pup!

PREVENTING PUPPY PROBLEMS

SOCIALISATION

Now that you have done all of the preparatory work and have helped your pup get accustomed to his new home and family, it is about time for you to have some fun! Socialising your Afghan Hound pup gives you the opportunity to show off your new friend, and your pup gets to reap the benefits of being an adorable furry creature that people will want to pet and, in general, think is absolutely precious!

Besides getting to know his new family, your puppy should be exposed to other people, animals and situations, but of course he must not come into close contact with dogs you don't know well until his course of injections is fully complete. This will help him become well adjusted as he grows up and less prone to being timid or fearful of the new things he will encounter. Your pup's socialisation began at the breeder's but now it is your responsibility to continue it. The socialisation he receives up until the age of 12 weeks is the most critical, as this is the time when he forms his impressions of the outside world. Be especially careful during the eight-to-ten-week period, also known as the fear period. The interaction he receives during this time should be gentle and reassuring. Lack of

SOCIALISATION

Thorough socialisation includes not only meeting new people but also being introduced to new experiences such as riding in the car, having his coat brushed, hearing the television, walking in a crowd—the list is

endless. The more your pup experiences, and the more positive the experiences are, the less of a shock and the less frightening it will be for your pup to encounter new things.

socialisation can manifest itself in fear and aggression as the dog grows up. He needs human contact, affection, handling and exposure to other animals.

Once your pup has received his necessary vaccinations, feel free to take him out and about (on his lead, of course). Walk him around the neighbourhood, take him on your daily errands, let people pet him, let him meet other dogs and pets, etc. Puppies do not have to try to make friends; there will be no shortage

CHEMICAL TOXINS

Scour your garage for potential puppy dangers. Remove weed killers, pesticides and antifreeze materials. Antifreeze is highly toxic and even a few drops can kill an adult dog. The sweet taste attracts the animal, who will quickly consume it from the floor or curbside.

of people who will want to introduce themselves. Just make sure that you carefully supervise each meeting and never force an Afghan to meet a stranger. If the neighbourhood children want to say hello, for example, that is great—children and pups most often make great companions. Sometimes an excited child can unintentionally handle a pup too roughly, or an overzealous pup can playfully nip a little too hard. You want to make socialisation experiences positive ones. What a pup learns during this very formative stage will affect

his attitude toward future encounters. You want your dog to be comfortable around everyone. A pup that has a bad experience with a child may grow up to be a dog that is shy around or aggressive toward children.

CONSISTENCY IN TRAINING

Dogs, being pack animals, naturally need a leader, or else they try to establish dominance in their packs. When you bring a dog into your family, the choice of who becomes the leader and who becomes the 'pack' is entirely up to you! Your pup's intuitive quest for dominance, coupled with the fact that he is an Afghan Hound, makes it difficult for owners to be 'top dog.' Afghans naturally treat humans as equals and do not respond to harsh discipline or 'unfair' treatment. A pup will definitely test the waters to see what he can and cannot do. Do not give in to those pleading eyes—stand your ground when it comes to disciplining the pup and make sure that all family members do the same. It will only confuse the pup when Mother tells him to get off the sofa when he is used to sitting up there with Father to watch the nightly news. Avoid discrepancies by having all members of the household decide on the rules before the pup even comes home...and be consistent in

'Can I have a taste?' It may be tempting to share a snack with your Afghan, but you don't want to turn a well-behaved pet into a beggar.

enforcing them! Early training shapes the dog's personality, so you cannot be unclear in what you expect.

COMMON PUPPY PROBLEMS

The best way to prevent puppy problems is to be proactive in stopping an undesirable behaviour as soon as it starts. The old saying 'You can't teach an old dog new tricks' does not necessarily hold true, but it is true that it is much easier to discourage bad behaviour in a young developing pup than to wait until the pup's bad behaviour becomes the adult dog's bad habit. There are some problems that are especially prevalent in puppies as they develop.

NIPPING

As puppies start to teethe, they feel the need to sink their teeth into anything available…unfortunately that includes your fingers, arms, hair and toes. You may find this behaviour cute for the first five seconds…until you feel just how sharp those puppy teeth are. This is something you want to discourage immediately and consistently with a firm 'No!' (or whatever number of firm 'No's' it takes for him to understand that you mean business). Then replace your finger with an appropriate chew toy. Whilst this behaviour is merely annoying

TOXIC PLANTS

Many plants can be toxic to dogs. If you see your dog carrying a piece of vegetation in his mouth, approach him in a quiet, disinterested manner, avoid eye contact, pet him and gradually remove the plant from his

mouth. Alternatively, offer him a treat and maybe he'll drop the plant on his own accord. Be sure no toxic plants are growing in your own garden.

when the dog is young, it can become dangerous as your Afghan Hound's adult teeth grow in and his jaws develop, and he continues to think it is acceptable to gnaw on human appendages. Your Afghan Hound does not mean any harm with a friendly nip, but he also does not know his own strength.

CRYING/WHINING

Your pup will often cry, whine, whimper, howl or make some type of commotion when he is left alone. This is basically his way of calling out for attention to make sure that you know he is

63

there and that you have not forgotten about him. He feels insecure when he is left alone, when you are out of the house and he is in his crate or when you are in another part of the house and he cannot see you. The noise he is making is an expression of the anxiety he feels at being alone, so he needs to be taught that being alone is okay. You are not actually training the dog to stop making noise, you are training him to feel comfortable when he is alone and thus removing the need for him to make the noise. This is where the crate with cosy bedding and a toy comes in handy. You want to know that he is safe when you are not there to supervise, and you know that he will be safe in his crate rather than roaming freely about the house. In order for the pup to stay in his crate without making a fuss, he needs to be comfortable in his crate. On that note, it is extremely important that the crate is never used as a form of punishment, or the pup will have a negative association with the crate.

Accustom the pup to the crate in short, gradually increasing time intervals in which you put him in the crate, maybe with a treat, and stay in the room with him. If he cries or makes a fuss, do not go to him, but stay in his sight. Gradually he will realise that staying in his

CHEWING TIPS

Chewing goes hand in hand with nipping in the sense that a teething puppy is always looking for a way to soothe his aching gums. In this case, instead of chewing on you, he may have taken a liking to your favourite shoe or something else which he should not be chewing. Again, realise that this is a normal canine behaviour that does not need to be discouraged, only redirected. Your pup just needs to be taught what is acceptable to chew on and what is off limits. Consistently tell him NO when you catch him chewing on something forbidden and give him a chew toy. Conversely, praise him when you catch him chewing on something appropriate. In this way you are discouraging the inappropriate behaviour and reinforcing the desired behaviour. The puppy chewing should stop after his adult teeth have come in, but an adult dog continues to chew for various reasons—perhaps because he is bored, perhaps to relieve tension or perhaps he just likes to chew. That is why it is important to redirect his chewing when he is still young.

crate is all right without your help, and it will not be so traumatic for him when you are not around. You may want to leave the radio on softly when you leave the house; the sound of human voices may be comforting to him.

EVERYDAY CARE OF YOUR
AFGHAN HOUND

DIETARY AND FEEDING CONSIDERATIONS

Today the choices of food for your Afghan Hound are many and varied. There are simply dozens of brands of food in all sorts of flavours and textures, ranging from puppy diets to those for seniors. There are even hypoallergenic and low-calorie diets available. Because your Afghan Hound's food has a bearing on coat, health and temperament, it is essential that the most suitable diet be selected for an Afghan Hound of his age. It is fair to say, however, that even dedicated owners can be somewhat perplexed by the enormous range of foods available. Only understanding what is best for your dog will help you reach a valued decision.

Dog foods are produced in three basic types: dried, semi-moist and tinned. Dried foods are useful for the cost-conscious for overall they tend to be less expensive than semi-moist or tinned. These contain the least fat and the most preservatives. In general tinned foods are made up of 60–70 percent water, whilst semi-moist ones often contain so much sugar that they are perhaps the least preferred by owners, even though their dogs seem to like them.

When selecting your dog's diet, three stages of development must be considered: the puppy stage, the adult stage and the senior or veteran stage.

PUPPY STAGE

Puppies instinctively want to suck milk from their mother's

DID YOU KNOW?

You must store your dried dog food carefully. Open packages of dog food quickly lose their vitamin value, usually within 90 days of being opened. Mould spores and vermin could also contaminate the food.

DID YOU KNOW?

A good test for proper diet is the colour, odour and firmness of your dog's stool. A healthy dog usually produces three semi-hard stools per day. The stools should have no unpleasant odour. They should be the same colour from excretion to excretion.

teats and a normal puppy will exhibit this behaviour from just a few moments following birth. If puppies do not attempt to suckle within the first half-hour or so, they should be encouraged to do so by placing them on the nipples, having selected ones with plenty of milk. This early milk supply is important in providing colostrum to protect the puppies during the first eight to ten weeks of their lives. Although a mother's milk is much better than any milk formula, despite there being some excellent ones available, if the puppies do not feed you will have to feed them yourself. For those with less experience, advice from a veterinary surgeon is important so that you feed not only the right quantity of milk but that of correct quality, fed at suitably frequent intervals, usually every two hours during the first few days of life.

Puppies should be allowed to nurse from their mothers for about the first six weeks, although from the third or fourth week you will have begun to introduce small portions of suitable solid food. Most breeders like to introduce alternate milk and meat meals initially, building up to weaning time.

By the time the puppies are seven or a maximum of eight weeks old, they should be fully weaned and fed solely on a proprietary puppy food. Selection of the most suitable, good-quality diet at this time is essential for a puppy's fastest growth rate is during the first year of life. Veterinary surgeons are usually able to offer advice in this regard and, although the frequency of meals will have been reduced over time, only when a young dog has reached the age of about 12 months should an adult diet be fed.

Puppy and junior diets should be well-balanced for the needs of your dog, so that except in certain circumstances additional vitamins, minerals and proteins will not be required.

It is always wise to start your puppy off on the food that has been fed by the breeder. You should have a full diet sheet and it is sensible to follow this, initially. It is also wise to take the diet sheet to your veterinary surgeon when you first take your puppy, so that you can discuss the puppy's diet with a professional. When selecting any all-in-one diet for puppies, do be guided by the veterinary surgeon as there are many on the market and the choice is not always easy.

ADULT DIETS

A dog is considered an adult when it has stopped growing, so in general the diet of an Afghan Hound can be changed to an adult one at about 10 to 12 months of age. Again you should rely upon your veterinary surgeon or dietary specialist to recommend an acceptable maintenance diet. Major dog food manufacturers specialise in this type of food, and it is just necessary for you to select the one best suited to your dog's needs. Active dogs may have different requirements than sedate dogs.

As your Afghan Hound grows you may wish to vary the diet. You can choose a quality all-in-one diet, fed to manufacturers specifications, or you can choose a natural diet. You may wish to opt for a combination of the two. In all cases the diet should be well-balanced and this is an aspect in which you can be guided by your vet. Being a dog with a hunting history, Afghan Hounds do welcome fresh meat in the diet along with wholemeal biscuit, although a source of good-quality fresh dog meat is not always readily available.

FOOD PREFERENCE

Selecting the best dried dog food is difficult. There is no majority consensus amongst veterinary scientists as to the value of nutrient analyses (protein, fat, fibre, moisture, ash, cholesterol, minerals, etc.). All agree that feeding trials are what matters, but you also have to consider the individual dog. Its

weight, age, activity and what pleases its taste, all must be considered. It is probably best to take the advice of your veterinary surgeon. Every dog's dietary requirements vary, even during the lifetime of a particular dog.

If your dog is fed a good dried food, it does not require supplements of meat or vegetables. Dogs do appreciate a little variety in their diets so you may choose to stay with the same brand, but vary the flavour. Alternatively you may wish to add a little flavoured stock to give a difference to the taste.

DID YOU KNOW?

Dog food must be at room temperature, neither too hot nor too cold. Fresh water, changed daily and served in a clean bowl, is mandatory, especially when feeding dried food. Never feed your dog from the

table while you are eating. Never feed your dog left-overs from your own meal. They usually contain too much fat and too much seasoning.

Dogs must chew their food. Hard pellets are excellent; soups and slurries are to be avoided.

Don't add left-overs or any extras to normal dog food. The normal food is usually balanced and adding something extra destroys the balance.

Except for age-related changes, dogs do not require dietary variations. They can be fed the same diet, day after day, without their becoming ill.

It is more convenient and appears more comfortable for Afghan Hounds to eat their meals from a raised surface; a low table is ideal. The snood, a tube of material used to protect the ear feathering from inadvertent chewing and food debris, is also recommended and highly favoured by most Afghan Hound owners.

Some Afghan Hounds seem to have poor appetites. It is generally best to resist the temptation to hand-feed your dog, unless all else has failed. Hand-feeding can be a habit that is easily picked up and hard to break. Veterinary advice should be sought if your Afghan Hound is not eating well. Although there may be nothing seriously wrong, it is always best to exclude this possibility.

Afghan Hounds kept in households where there are other dogs may be less inclined to refuse food; however, they should always be fed separately from other dogs to counteract jealousy.

The Afghan Hound is not a dog with a deep abdomen (deep-bodied breeds are often considered to be prone to gastric torsion or bloat). However, it is always a sensible precaution not to feed your dog immediately before or after exercise and to avoid large meals or dried food that has not been well soaked, according to

What are you feeding your dog?

Read the label on your dog food. Many dog foods only advise what 50—55% of the contents are, leaving the other 45% in doubt.

50%

40%

30%

20%

10%

0%

1.3% Calcium

1.6% Fatty Acids

4.6% Crude Fibre

11% Moisture

14% Crude Fat

22% Crude Protein

45.5% ? ? ?

GRAIN-BASED DIETS

Some less expensive dog foods are based on grains and other plant proteins. Whilst these products may appear to be attractively priced, many breeders prefer a diet based on animal proteins and believe that they are more

conducive to your dog's health. Many grain-based diets rely on soy protein that may cause flatulence (passing gas).

There are many cases, however, when your dog might require a special diet. These special requirements should only be recommended by your veterinary surgeon.

the manufacturer's specification. Gastric torsion is a matter of extreme urgency, characterised by swelling of the abdomen with a very bloated look. Immediate veterinary attention can save lives.

SENIOR DIETS

As dogs get older, their metabolism changes. The older dog usually exercises less, moves more slowly and sleeps more. This change in lifestyle and physiological performance requires a change in diet. Since these changes take place slowly, they might not be recognisable. What is easily recognisable is weight gain. By continuing to feed your dog an adult-maintenance diet when it is slowing down metabolically, your dog will gain weight. Obesity in an older dog compounds the health problems that already accompany old age.

As your dog gets older, few of their organs function up to par. The kidneys slow down and the intestines become less efficient. These age-related factors are best handled with a change in diet and a change in feeding schedule to give smaller portions that are more easily digested.

There is no single best diet for every older dog. Whilst many dogs do well on light or senior diets, other dogs do better on puppy diets or other special premium diets such as lamb and rice. Be sensitive to your senior Afghan Hound's diet and this will help control other problems that may arise with your old friend.

WATER

Just as your dog needs proper nutrition from his food, water is an essential 'nutrient' as well.

Water keeps the dog's body properly hydrated and promotes normal function of the body's systems. During housebreaking it is necessary to keep an eye on how much water your Afghan Hound is drinking, but once he is reliably trained he should have access to clean fresh water at all times. Make sure that the dog's water bowl is clean, and change the water often, making sure that water is always available for your dog, especially if you feed dried food.

EXERCISE

Exercise is something of an interesting subject in Afghan Hounds. This is a sighthound and, just as you would expect a working sheepdog to display some of its instincts within a

field of sheep, you can expect an Afghan Hound to display some of the instincts of its forebears when faced with an open field with far horizons. To understand an Afghan Hound, you need to look at exercise with their viewpoint in mind. This is an agile, free-spirited dog who loves to run. In addition an Afghan Hound, being a sighthound, looks into the distance for interest's sake, with the gimlet eye of an eagle. If you combine an Afghan Hound without a lead with an exercise area without boundary fences, you are heading for a spot of trouble. An Afghan Hound has little sense of the passage of time, when enjoying itself. These dogs are capable of lying on a sofa all day, but give them a sense of freedom and they may stay out for many hours. Generally, in my experience, they will return, but sometimes not until you have been quite distracted about them.

It is a great deal easier to

On-lead walks provide both dog and owner with exercise.

Your Afghan should always have clean, fresh water available.

71

All members of the family can participate in activities with the Afghan Hound. Children can take the dog for walks, provided that the children are taught to handle the dog on lead and the dog has been trained to heel.

accept the innate traits of your Afghan Hound and to realise that it is not a case of the dog's being difficult or stupid for running away from you. Therefore, if you wish to live peaceably with your Afghan Hound and if you do not wish to be wandering for hours searching for your dog or answering questions from the police about what your dog has been doing whilst it has been out, it is advisable to prevent the escape before it happens.

It is not possible to satisfy the exercise needs of an Afghan Hound with purely on-lead walking; it is necessary also to give these dogs free running. Therefore you will need to find a

The Afghan Hound is a breed known for speed and stamina, as illustrated by this graceful racer. An Afghan owner must be committed to providing his dog with enough activity and exercise.

safe, fenced area in which you can allow your dog to run freely, which will prevent the dog from running out of your range. Afghan Hounds have a tremendous turn of speed and love to run together with another of their own breed. Watching Afghan Hounds run is an exhilarating and awe-inspiring experience. An ideal place to allow free running is a well-fenced grass area, as some Afghan Hounds will easily and gracefully clear fencing of 1.5 metres or so. If your garden space allows, you may wish to fence a large running area with 3-metre chain-link fencing.

From an early age it is important to give your puppy something pleasurable to which to return when you call. Some Afghan Hounds are disinterested in titbits, so praise and a bit of fun after the lead is back on are important for them. In this way some Afghan Hounds can be taught to reliably return when called by their owners, thus making it easier to provide them with the off-lead exercise that they need.

Afghan Hound racing is a popular sport amongst many Afghan Hound owners. Racing, under safely controlled conditions, can be excellent exercise for these hounds and good fun for both dog and owner. Your local or national Afghan Hound club will be able to advise

WALKING LIKE A PRO

For many people it is difficult to imagine putting your dog's well being in someone else's hands, but if you are unable to give your dog his necessary exercise breaks, hiring a professional dog walker may be a good idea. Dog walkers offer your dog exercise, a chance to work off energy and companionship—all things that keep your dog healthy. Seek referrals from your veterinary surgeon, breeder or groomer to find a reputable dog walker.

you of racing opportunities in your area.

Exercise is vital to the health and happiness of your Afghan Hound, so you need to be sure you know how you are going to provide this, safely, before taking one of these noble and unique dogs into your family.

Bear in mind that an overweight dog should never be suddenly over-exercised; instead, he should be allowed to increase exercise slowly. Not only is exercise essential to keep the dog's body fit, it is essential to his mental well-being. A bored dog will find something to do, which often manifests itself in some type of destructive behaviour. In this sense, it is essential for the owner's mental well-being as well!

Your local pet shop will carry a variety of grooming tool for you to choose from.

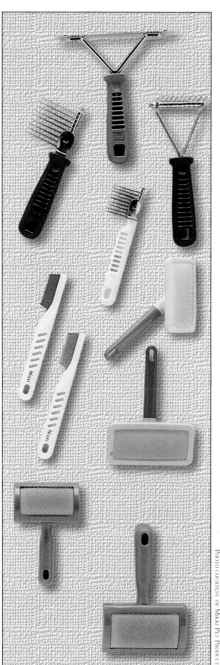

GROOMING

The coat pattern of the Afghan Hound is unique and provides something of a challenge to its owner. This breed requires frequent, thorough grooming and you should be very sure that you will wish to take this on, if you are going to acquire an Afghan Hound. A well-groomed Afghan Hound, in full coat, is a most beautiful sight, but it requires hard work and dedication.

GROOMING THE PUPPY

It is essential that you should begin to groom your Afghan Hound as a puppy. Using a soft bristle or bristle and nylon brush on a pneumatic rubber base, work right over the puppy, to ensure

GROOMING EQUIPMENT

How much grooming equipment you purchase will depend on how much grooming you are going to do. Here are some basics:

- Natural bristle brush
- Bristle & nylon brush on a pneumatic rubber base
- Metal comb
- Scissors
- Blaster
- Rubber mat
- Dog shampoo
- Showerhead attachment
- Ear cleaner
- Cotton wipes
- Towels
- Nail clippers

The Afghan's coat should first be thoroughly wet before applying shampoo.

The stream of water is directed away from the dog's eyes and ears.

Shampoo is then applied to the coat and worked into a lather.

Any excess water in the coat should be squeezed out. Be alert for soap suds, which indicate that the dog has not been rinsed thoroughly.

Stand back! As soon as you release your grip on the wet dog, he'll shake the water from his coat.

Brushing and combing will detangle the coat as it is drying.

that the whole body is brushed. At this stage you are really just keeping the coat in good condition and getting the puppy used to what is to become a regular routine. It is probably best to stand the puppy on a safe, non-slip surface for grooming. Keep one hand on the puppy to prevent dangerous bids for freedom. Later you will need to do this with your adult Afghan to enable you to access all areas of the coat.

Using a high-quality blaster, the coat should be dried in sections, straightening each section as you go.

Using a lead to assist you in controlling the puppy is helpful. In the beginning, it is usually easier to have someone else assist you to keep the puppy still. At the time of grooming do take the opportunity of getting the puppy used to having the ears, teeth and nails attended to, as it will help you later if the dog accepts this as part of life.

Regular bathing is also a good routine for your puppy to learn, using a good-quality puppy shampoo. Always use a conditioning rinse after rinsing out the shampoo, as this will promote good condition of the coat. After careful bathing and final rinsing with clean water, always dry your puppy, fully, in a warm, draught-free atmosphere. It is advisable to brush the coat as the puppy dries, so that the hair dries straight and hangs well. Later this has the added advantage of keeping the coat from tangling again quite so quickly.

When your puppy's coat starts to grow, grooming will become steadily more time-consuming. The natural Afghan Hound coat pattern is, nowadays, not usually evident until the dog is older, if ever. However, some puppies and youngsters will have naturally 'bare' pasterns and a saddle, from an early age. These dogs will often, but not always, also have a lighter and therefore easier to manage silky coat. They will also often be more likely to lose a lot of this silky coat at times of coat change, such as after seasons, in females. Bare pasterns is a term used to describe the close, sharper hair type, the pastern is not actually devoid of coat altogether. The saddle coat in its natural form is a close, hard, shorter coat. When this saddle area does occur it may be discernible in the youngster or may not appear until the first major coat change at around 9 to 18 months. As the Afghan Hound coat grows, it lengthens steadily until a stage is reached when it is frequently tangling together. At this stage you will probably need to groom the coat fully every day, or every other day, or it will easily become matted.

BRUSHING

The Afghan Hound has fine and relatively sensitive skin, and the dog may be easily hurt when you are brushing the coat if you are not careful and gentle. Do remember this as the dog should not be expected to experience discomfort when being groomed.

When brushing the longer Afghan Hound coat, you will need to work systematically over the coat, turning the hair back to expose the roots of the lower layers. The use of hair clips to hold back the long coat and expose the underlying layers of coat can be very helpful when brushing the mature Afghan Hound. Brush in sweeping strokes with the lie of the coat from root to tip of the hair shafts. If you come to any matted or tangled areas, gently tease these

GROOMING TIP

Once you are sure that the dog is thoroughly rinsed, squeeze the excess water out of the coat with your hand and dry him with a heavy towel. You may choose to use a blaster on his coat or just let it dry naturally. In cold weather, never allow your dog outside with a wet coat.

There are 'dry bath' products on the market, which are sprays and powders intended for spot cleaning, that can be used between regular baths, if necessary. They are not substitutes for regular baths, but they are easy to use for touch-ups as they do not require rinsing.

out, using the finger and thumb of each hand. You may also wish to use a proprietary grooming spray to assist in easing the tangles out. Generally the best brush to use is still a pure bristle or bristle and nylon brush on a pneumatic rubber base. You may also wish to use a metal pin brush with a pneumatic rubber base; those brushes with blunted ends to the pins cause the least discomfort to the dog. Do remember that the metal pins will be harder on the skin and more damaging to the coat of the Afghan, so use this type of brush gently. The advantage is that the metal pins will groom through the coat more quickly so the number of brush strokes on the dog's skin will be reduced.

It is generally better to groom the Afghan prior to bathing as the washing of the coat renders any matted areas more difficult to clear. However, when you have bathed the dog, it is necessary to groom the coat again, thoroughly, to leave the coat in the best possible condition. If the coat is very dirty or sticky you will probably find that bathing before any brushing will cause the least damage to the coat. Any twigs, seeds or other debris that may have been picked up by the coat during exercise should be removed promptly as they will cause discomfort to the dog and matting of the coat.

BATHING AND DRYING

When bathing an Afghan Hound it is always sensible to try to minimise the tangling potential of the bathing process by gently working the shampoo through the coat without rubbing. By diluting the shampoo with water, easier application of the shampoo is possible. It is also generally easier to dampen the dog's coat with clear water prior to applying any shampoo. Don't forget to use comfortably warm water for your dog when applying shampoo or rinsing. With some shampoos, such as specific treatment shampoos, it is necessary to follow instructions closely to obtain the benefits required. The method of gently working the coat without rubbing is also used for rinsing and applying the conditioner prior to the final rinsing. Diluting the conditioner with water is helpful for ease of

GROOMING TIP

The use of human soap products like shampoo, bubble bath and hand soap can be damaging to a dog's coat and skin. Human products are too strong and remove the protective oils coating the dog's hair and skin (making him water-resistant). Use only shampoo made especially for dogs and you may like to use a medicated shampoo, which will always help to keep external parasites at bay.

If a knot is discovered, the hairs should first be detangled by hand.

Next, use a brush to remove the tangle.

Comb or brush gently until the hairs are perfectly separated.

Since the hairs on
the face are short,
only a damp cloth
is necessary to
clean it.

The feathering on
the ears is brushed
and dried with the
blaster.

Hair clips or
barrettes can be
used to section the
hair for the final
brushing.

application, although you may wish to apply the conditioner in a more concentrated solution directly into any tangled areas, as this can help in easing the tangles out during grooming. The use of a powerful showerhead will allow the coat to be rinsed with the lie of the coat, thus promoting tangle prevention. The face can usually be best cleaned by the use of a dampened piece of towelling. When washing and rinsing the head and neck, ensure that the flow of water runs away from the face and especially the eyes.

After bathing, try to minimise tangling by gently squeezing the water out of the coat and then gently squeezing the coat dry with the towel, rather than rubbing the coat dry, as you might with a shorter coated breed. Many people like to use a large free-standing dryer to dry the coat more quickly and to encourage the hair to hang straight and tangle less quickly. Many experienced Afghan Hound owners have a weekly routine of bathing and blow drying their adult Afghan Hounds. Despite this frequency, the whole routine can take two hours or more from start to finish. If you are going to adopt this routine, which hopefully enables the dogs always to remain in near tangle-free condition, you will need to use a good quality, conditioning

dog shampoo and a quality dog-specific conditioning rinse. A conditioning spray is also useful to spray into the coat whilst it is drying. It is hard to recommend a shampoo suitable to all Afghan Hound coats, as there are various types of coat in the breed. Some coats are naturally relatively oily, for instance, and some are dry and very fine and fly-away. You may have to try a few shampoos to arrive at the best one for your dog; it is also useful to take advice from the breeder.

GROOMING THE SHOW DOG

If you intend to show your Afghan Hound, it is essential that you familiarise yourself with the rules regarding the preparation of dogs for exhibition that may differ with country to country. For instance, it may not be permitted to leave a residue in the coat that would be deemed to alter the texture or colour of the coat. Failure to heed these regulations could lead to disqualification of your dog from any prizes won. Nevertheless, most exhibitors would advocate the use of conditioning treatments between shows, providing that they are washed out of the coat prior to attending a show.

MORE GROOMING TIPS

Grooming an Afghan Hound is an acquired art that you will be able to develop over the years of

Pre-show grooming. Afghan Hounds are groomed right before being shown so they look their best in the ring.

owning your dog. This means that you will improve with experience and, by developing a technique with your dog, grooming time will probably be reduced. Also, with age, most Afghan Hounds' coats become easier to manage and less prone to the frequent tangling that occurs during the adolescent stage.

In adult Afghan Hounds the ear feathering grows long and heavy. This coat can be vulnerable to chewing as the dog eats. To counteract this problem, many Afghan Hound owners use a snood or special material protector for the coat. Snoods can be put onto the dog prior to

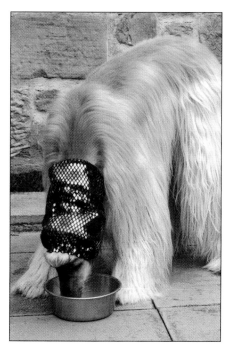

The use of a snood protects the feathering on the ears from falling into the food bowl as the dog eats.

83

eating and should always be removed promptly after the meal is eaten. Snoods are made of rectangles of material, sewn into a tube, with light elastic shirring at intervals, horizontally. These safely and gently hold all the head hair of the dog within them. Snoods can be readily purchased at specialist dog shows or local or national Afghan Hound club events. They can also be made at home, but sizing is critical. If they are too small they will be uncomfortable for the dog and damaging to the coat and, if they are too big, they will slip over the dog's eyes whilst eating.

Adult Afghan Hound males sometimes dampen the coats on their legs whilst passing urine. This can also be counteracted by the use of special dog coats that can be bought through Afghan Hound clubs and their shows. Shower-proofed dog coats are also available to use for lightly exercising your Afghan Hound in very wet weather. These are ideal if you want to arrive at a dog show with the dog in dry condition on a wet day. It would be unwise to use a dog coat for your dog during free running as accidents could happen if the dog's feet or limbs became entangled within the coat.

The coat of the Afghan Hound should not require trimming in any way. One of the most beautiful aspects of the breed is the natural coat pattern, with the smooth face and short saddle coat combined with the long, silky body coat. Some people do try to trim the coat on the back, should the dog not acquire a natural coat pattern, but this invariably looks artificial and would probably be best avoided. To add shine to the saddle of your Afghan Hound, you can use a chamois pad to buff the coat in the direction of the lie of the hairs.

Should your Afghan Hound become seriously matted, it would probably be kindest to the dog to have the coat trimmed or clipped and to start again with the coat short and re-grow it. It is extremely tedious and painful to the Afghan Hound to have a heavily matted coat groomed, and the option of professional trimming is, in my opinion, by far the best one in this case. However, it is always best to prevent the coat from getting seriously matted by undertaking regular, thorough grooming. An Afghan Hound does not, generally, look very attractive when the coat is very short but this is certainly preferable to an unhappy, matted dog and an owner who is full of guilt about his dog's felted coat. Once the coat is trimmed or clipped off, it will take a number of years to recover its full length. You should not trim the coat of your

Afghan Hound if you wish to show your dog.

If you are having problems with grooming your Afghan Hound's coat, it is best to seek the advice of the breeder of your dog. If this is not possible, an Afghan Hound exhibitor or an experienced owner would generally be happy to give advice that would help you and your dog.

EAR CLEANING

The ears should be kept clean without any excess hair. Fortunately, Afghan Hounds do not usually have a lot of hair inside their ears. Ears can be cleaned with a cotton wipe and ear powder made especially for dogs. Be on the lookout for any signs of infection or ear mite infestation. If your Afghan Hound has been shaking his head or scratching at his ears frequently, this usually indicates a problem. If his ears have an unusual odour, this is a sure sign of mite infestation or infection, and a signal to have his ears checked by the veterinary surgeon.

NAIL CLIPPING

Your Afghan Hound should be accustomed to having his nails trimmed at an early age, since it will be part of your maintenance routine throughout his life. Not only does it look nicer, but long, sharp nails can scratch someone unintentionally. Also, a long nail

The ears should be cleaned on a regular basis with a cotton wipe and ear powder.

You can learn to clip your dog's nails yourself with special clippers made just for use on dogs.

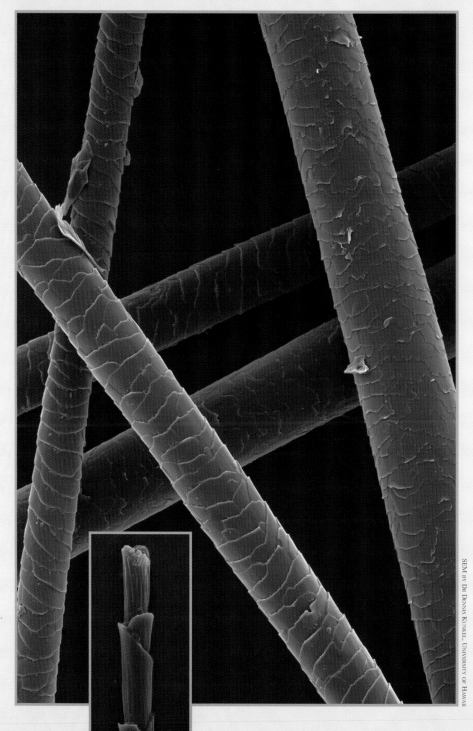

Normal hairs of a dog enlarged 200 times original size. The cuticle (outer covering) is clean and healthy. Unlike human hair that grows from the base, dog's hair also grows from the end, as shown in the inset. Scanning electron micrographs by Dr Dennis Kunkel, University of Hawaii.

has a better chance of ripping and bleeding, or causing the feet to spread. A good rule of thumb is that if you can hear your dog's nails clicking on the floor when he walks, his nails are too long.

Before you start cutting, make sure you can identify the 'quick' in each nail. The quick is a blood vessel that runs through the centre of each nail and grows rather close to the end. It will bleed if accidentally cut, which will be quite painful for the dog as it contains nerve endings. Keep some type of clotting agent on hand, such as a styptic pencil or styptic powder (the type used for shaving). This will stop the bleeding quickly when applied to the end of the cut nail. Do not panic if this happens, just stop the bleeding and talk soothingly to your dog. Once he has calmed down, move on to the next nail. It is better to clip a little at a time, particularly with black-nailed dogs.

Hold your pup steady as you begin trimming his nails; you do not want him to make any sudden movements or run away. Talk to him soothingly and stroke him as you clip. Holding his foot in your hand, simply take off the end of each nail in one quick clip. You can purchase nail clippers that are specially made for dogs; you can probably find them wherever you buy pet or grooming supplies.

Nail Maintenance

Nail Casing

Quick

Cut Line

Clip only the bottom portion of the nail, avoiding the quick. If you cut into the quick, the nail will bleed and the dog will experience pain. A styptic pencil will stop the bleeding. Reassure the injured dog by talking quietly to him.

Dark-Coloured Nails

With black or dark nails, where the quick is not easy to see, it's best to clip only the tip of the nail or to use a file.

Light-Coloured Nails

In light-coloured nails, clipping is much simpler because you can see the vein (or quick) that grows inside the casing.

87

DID YOU KNOW?

A dog that spends a lot of time outside on a hard surface, such as cement or pavement, will have his nails naturally worn down and may not need to have them trimmed as often, except maybe in the colder months when he is not outside as much. Regardless, it is best

to get your dog accustomed to this procedure at an early age so that he is used to it. Some dogs are especially sensitive about having their feet touched, but if a dog has experienced it since he was young, he should not be bothered by it.

TRAVELLING WITH YOUR DOG

CAR TRAVEL
You should accustom your Afghan Hound to riding in a car at an early age. You may or may not take him in the car often, but at the very least he will need to go to the vet and you do not want these trips to be traumatic for the dog or troublesome for you. The safest way for a dog to ride in the car is in his crate. If he uses a crate in the house, you can use the same crate for travel.

Put the pup in the crate and see how he reacts. If he seems uneasy, you can have a passenger hold him on his lap whilst you drive. Another option is a specially made safety harness for dogs, which straps the dog in much like a seat belt. Do not let the dog roam loose in the vehicle—this is very dangerous! If you should stop short, your dog can be thrown and injured. If the dog starts climbing on you and pestering you whilst you are driving, you will not be able to concentrate on the road. It is an unsafe situation for everyone—human and canine.

For long trips, be prepared to stop to let the dog relieve himself. Bring along whatever you need to clean up after him. You should take along some paper kitchen towels and perhaps some old towelling for use should he have an accident in the car or suffer from travel sickness.

AIR TRAVEL
Whilst it is possible to take a dog on a flight within Britain, this is fairly unusual and advance permission is always required. The dog will be required to travel in a fibreglass crate and you should always

check in advance with the airline regarding specific requirements. To help the dog be at ease, put one of his favourite toys in the crate with him. Do not feed the dog for at least six hours before the trip to minimise his need to relieve himself. However, certain regulations specify that water must always be made available to the dog in the crate.

Make sure your dog is properly identified and that your contact information appears on his ID tags and on his crate. Animals travel in a different area of the plane than human passengers so every rule must be strictly adhered to so as to prevent the

risk of getting separated from your dog.

BOARDING

So you want to take a family holiday—and you want to include all members of the

> **TRAVEL TIP**
>
> If you are going on a long motor trip with your dog, be sure the hotels are dog friendly. Many hotels do not accept dogs. Also take along some ice that can be thawed and offered to your dog if he becomes overheated. Most dogs like to lick ice.

Your Afghan Hound must be secure in his crate during any transport by car. A dog loose in the car is dangerous for all concerned.

89

family. You would probably make arrangements for accommodation ahead of time anyway, but this is especially important when travelling with a dog. You do not want to make an overnight stop at the only place around for miles and find out that they do not allow dogs. Also, you do not want to reserve a place for your family without confirming that you are travelling with a dog because if it is against their policy you may not have a place to stay.

Alternatively, if you are travelling and choose not to bring your Afghan Hound, you will have to make arrangements for him whilst you are away. Some options are to take him to a neighbour's house to stay whilst you are gone, to have a trusted neighbour pop in often or stay at your house, or bring your dog to a reputable boarding kennel. If you choose to board him at a kennel, you should visit in advance to see the facilities provided, how clean they are and where the dogs are kept. Talk to some of the employees and see how they treat the dogs—do they spend time with the dogs, play with them, exercise them, etc.? Also find out the kennel's policy on vaccinations and what they require. This is for all of the dogs' safety, since when dogs are kept together, there is a greater risk of diseases being passed from dog to dog.

IDENTIFICATION

If your dog gets lost, he is not able to ask for directions home.

Identification tags fastened to the collar give important information—the dog's name, the owner's name, the owner's address and a telephone number where the owner

can be reached. This makes it easy for whom ever finds the dog to contact the owner and arrange to have the dog returned. An added advantage is that a person will be more likely to approach a lost dog who has ID tags on his collar; it tells the person that this is somebody's pet rather than a stray. This is the easiest and fastest method of identification provided that the tags stay on the collar and the collar stays on the dog.

IDENTIFICATION

Your Afghan Hound is your valued companion and friend. That is why you always keep a close eye on him and you have made sure that he cannot escape from the garden or wriggle out of his collar and run away from you. However, accidents can happen and there may come a time when your dog unexpectedly gets separated from you. If this unfortunate event should occur, the first thing on your mind will be finding him. Proper identification, including an ID tag, a tattoo and possibly a microchip, will increase the chances of his being returned to you safely and quickly.

TRAVEL TIP

The most extensive travel you do with your dog may be limited to trips to the veterinary surgeon's office—or you may decide to bring him along for

long distances when the family goes on holiday. Whichever the case, it is important to consider your dog's safety while travelling.

DID YOU KNOW?

As puppies become more and more expensive, especially those puppies of high quality for showing and/or breeding, they have a greater chance of being stolen. The usual collar dog tag is, of course, easily removed. But there are two techniques that have become widely used for identification.

The puppy microchip implantation involves the injection of a small microchip, about the size of a corn kernel, under the skin of the dog. If your dog shows up at a clinic or shelter, or is offered for resale under less than savoury circumstances, it can be positively identified by the microchip. The microchip is scanned and a registry quickly identifies you as the owner. This is not only protection against theft, but should the dog run away or go chasing a squirrel and get lost, you have a fair chance of getting it back.

Tattooing is done on various parts of the dog, from its belly to its cheeks. The number tattooed can be your telephone number or any other number which you can easily memorise. When professional dog thieves see a tattooed dog, they usually lose interest in it. Both microchipping and tattooing can be done at your local veterinary clinic. For the safety of our dogs, no laboratory facility or dog broker will accept a tattooed dog as stock.

DID YOU KNOW?

If you start with a normal, healthy dog and give him time, patience and some carefully executed lessons, you will reap the rewards of that training

for the life of the dog. And what a life it will be! The two of you will find immeasurable pleasure in the companionship you have built together with love, respect and understanding.

Living with an untrained dog is a lot like owning a piano that you do not know how to play—it is a nice object to look at but it does not do much more than that to bring you pleasure. Now try taking piano lessons and suddenly the piano comes alive and brings forth magical sounds and rhythms that set your heart singing and your body swaying.

The same is true with your Afghan Hound. Any dog is a big responsibility and if not trained sensibly may develop unacceptable behaviour that annoys you or could even cause family friction.

To train your Afghan Hound, you may like to enrol in an obedience class. Teach him good manners as you learn how and why he behaves the way he does. Find out how to communicate with your dog and how to recognise and understand his communications with you. Suddenly the dog takes on a new role in your life—he is clever, interesting, well behaved and fun to be with. He demonstrates his bond of devotion to you daily. In other words, your Afghan Hound does wonders for your ego because he constantly reminds you that you are the human he has chosen to count as his own!

Those involved with teaching dog obedience and counselling owners about their dogs' behaviour have discovered some interesting facts about dog ownership. For example, training dogs when they are puppies results in the highest rate of success in developing well-mannered and well-adjusted adult dogs. Training an older dog, from six months to six years of age, can produce almost equal results providing that the owner accepts the dog's slower rate of learning capability and is

DID YOU KNOW?

To a dog's way of thinking, your hands are like his mouth in terms of a defence mechanism. If you squeeze him too tightly, he might just bite you because that would be his normal response. This is not aggressive biting and, although all biting should be discouraged, you need the discipline in learning how to handle your dog.

willing to work patiently to help the dog succeed at developing to his fullest potential. Unfortunately, many owners of untrained adult dogs lack the patience factor, so they do not persist until their dogs are successful at learning particular behaviours.

Training a puppy aged 10 to 16 weeks (20 weeks at the most) is like working with a dry sponge in a pool of water. The pup soaks up whatever you show him and constantly looks for more things to do and learn. At this early age, his body is not yet producing hormones, and therein lies the reason for such a high rate of success. Without hormones, he is focused on his owners and not particularly interested in investigating other places, dogs, people, etc. You are his leader: his provider of food, water, shelter and security. He latches onto you

Training produces an Afghan Hound who is a well-trained member of the family.

93

Training a dog is a life experience. Many parents admit that much of what they know about raising children they

learned from caring for their dogs. Dogs respond to love, fairness and guidance, just as children do. Become a good dog owner and you may become an even better parent.

curiosity emerges and he begins to investigate the world around him. It is at this time when you may notice that the untrained dog begins to wander away from you and even ignore your commands to stay close. When this behaviour becomes a problem, the owner has two choices: get rid of the dog or train him. It is strongly urged that you choose the latter option.

There are usually classes within a reasonable distance from the owner's home, but you also do much to train your dog yourself. Sometimes there are classes available but the tuition is too costly. Whatever the circumstances, the solution to the problem of lack of lesson availability lies within the pages of this book.

This chapter is devoted to helping you train your Afghan Hound at home. If the recommended procedures are followed faithfully, you may expect positive results that will prove rewarding to both you and your dog.

Whether your new charge is a puppy or a mature adult, the methods of teaching and the techniques we use in training basic behaviours are the same. After all, no dog, whether puppy or adult, likes harsh or inhumane methods. All creatures, however, respond

and wants to stay close. He will usually follow you from room to room, will not let you out of his sight when you are outdoors with him, and will respond in like manner to the people and animals you encounter. If you greet a friend warmly, he will greet the person as well. If, however, you are hesitant, even anxious, about the approach of a stranger, he will respond accordingly.

Once the puppy begins to produce hormones, his natural

favourably to gentle motivational methods and sincere praise and encouragement. Now let us get started.

HOUSEBREAKING

You can train a puppy to relieve itself wherever you choose, but this must be somewhere suitable. You should bear in mind from the outset that when your puppy is old enough to go out in public places, any canine deposits must be removed at once. You will always have to carry with you a small plastic bag or 'poop-scoop.'

Outdoor training includes such surfaces as grass, soil or earth and cement. Indoor training usually means training your dog to newspaper.

When deciding on the surface and location that you will want your Afghan Hound to use, be sure it is going to be permanent. Training your dog to grass and then changing your mind two months later is extremely difficult for both dog and owner.

Next, choose the command you will use each and every time you want your puppy to void. 'Be quick,' 'Hurry up' and 'Toilet' are examples of commands commonly used by dog owners.

Get in the habit of giving the puppy your chosen relief command before you take him

DID YOU KNOW?

Dogs do not understand our language. They can be trained to react to a certain sound, at a certain volume. If you say 'No, Oliver' in a very soft pleasant voice it will not have the same meaning as 'No, Oliver!!' when you shout it as loud as you can. You should never use the dog's name during a reprimand, just the command NO!! Since dogs don't understand words, comics often use dogs trained with opposite meanings. Thus, when the comic commands his dog to SIT the dog will stand up, and vice versa.

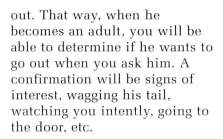

OBEDIENCE CLASS

A basic obedience beginner's class usually lasts for six to eight weeks. Dog and owner attend an hour-long lesson once a week and practise for a few minutes, several times a day, each day at home. If done properly, the whole procedure will result in a well-mannered dog and an owner who delights in living with a pet that is eager to please and enjoys doing things with his owner.

out. That way, when he becomes an adult, you will be able to determine if he wants to go out when you ask him. A confirmation will be signs of interest, wagging his tail, watching you intently, going to the door, etc.

PUPPY'S NEEDS

A puppy needs to relieve himself after play periods, after each meal, after he has been sleeping and any time he indicates that he is looking for a place to urinate or defecate.

The urinary and intestinal tract muscles of very young puppies are not fully developed. Therefore, like human babies, puppies need to relieve themselves frequently.

Take your puppy out often—every hour for an eight-week-old, for example, and always immediately after sleeping and eating. The older the puppy, the less often he will need to relieve himself. Finally, as a mature healthy adult, he will require only three to five relief trips per day.

HOUSING

Since the type of housing and control you provide for your puppy has a direct relationship on the success of housetraining, we consider the various aspects of both before we begin training.

Bringing a new puppy home and turning him loose in your house can be compared to turning a child loose in a sports arena and telling the child that the place is all his! The sheer enormity of the place would be too much for him to handle.

Instead, offer the puppy clearly defined areas where he can play, sleep, eat and live. A room of the house where the family gathers is the most obvious choice. Puppies are social animals and need to feel a part of the pack right from the start. Hearing your voice, watching you whilst you are doing things and smelling you nearby are all positive reinforcers that he is now a member of your pack. Usually a family room, the kitchen or a nearby adjoining breakfast area

CANINE DEVELOPMENT SCHEDULE

It is important to understand how and at what age a puppy develops into adulthood. If you are a puppy owner, consult the following Canine Development Schedule to determine the stage of development your puppy is currently experiencing. This knowledge will help you as you work with the puppy in the weeks and months ahead.

Period	Age	Characteristics
FIRST TO THIRD	**BIRTH TO SEVEN WEEKS**	Puppy needs food, sleep and warmth, and responds to simple and gentle touching. Needs mother for security and disciplining. Needs littermates for learning and interacting with other dogs. Pup learns to function within a pack and learns pack order of dominance. Begin socialising with adults and children for short periods. Begins to become aware of its environment.
FOURTH	**EIGHT TO TWELVE WEEKS**	Brain is fully developed. Needs socialising with outside world. Remove from mother and littermates. Needs to change from canine pack to human pack. Human dominance necessary. Fear period occurs between 8 and 16 weeks. Avoid fright and pain.
FIFTH	**THIRTEEN TO SIXTEEN WEEKS**	Training and formal obedience should begin. Less association with other dogs, more with people, places, situations. Period will pass easily if you remember this is pup's change-to-adolescence time. Be firm and fair. Flight instinct prominent. Permissiveness and over-disciplining can do permanent damage. Praise for good behaviour.
JUVENILE	**FOUR TO EIGHT MONTHS**	Another fear period about 7 to 8 months of age. It passes quickly, but be cautious of fright and pain. Sexual maturity reached. Dominant traits established. Dog should understand sit, down, come and stay by now.

NOTE: THESE ARE APPROXIMATE TIME FRAMES. ALLOW FOR INDIVIDUAL DIFFERENCES IN PUPPIES.

is ideal for providing safety and security for both puppy and owner.

Within that room there should be a smaller area which the puppy can call his own. An alcove, a wire or fibreglass dog crate or a fenced (not boarded!) corner from which he can view the activities of his new family will be fine. The size of the area or crate is the key factor here. The area must be large enough for the puppy to lie down and stretch out as well as stand up without rubbing his head on the top, yet it must be small enough so that he cannot relieve himself at one end and sleep at the other without coming into contact with his droppings until fully trained to relieve himself outside.

Dogs are, by nature, clean animals and will not remain

TRAINING TIP

Never train your dog, puppy or adult, when you are angry or in a sour mood. Dogs are very sensitive to human feelings, especially anger, and if your dog senses that you are angry or upset, he will connect your anger with his training and learn to resent or fear his training sessions.

close to their relief areas unless forced to do so. In those cases, they then become dirty dogs and usually remain that way for life.

The designated area should be lined with clean bedding and contain a toy. Water must always be available, in a non-spill container.

CONTROL

By control, we mean helping the puppy to create a lifestyle pattern that will be compatible to that of his human pack (YOU!). Just as we guide little children to learn our way of life, we must show the puppy when it is time to play, eat, sleep, exercise and even entertain himself.

Your puppy should always sleep in his crate. He should also learn that, during times of household confusion and excessive human activity such as at breakfast when family members are preparing for the

Once the Afghan has been crate-trained, he will enjoy resting in his crate and will spend time there willingly.

day, he can play by himself in relative safety and comfort in his designated area. Whenever you leave the puppy alone, he should understand exactly where he is to stay. Puppies are chewers. They cannot tell the difference between lamp cords, television wires, shoes, table legs, etc. Chewing into a television wire, for example, can be fatal to the puppy whilst a shorted wire can start a fire in the house.

If the puppy chews on the arm of the chair when he is alone, you will probably discipline him angrily when you get home. Thus, he makes the association that your coming home means he is going to be punished. (He will not remember chewing the chair and is incapable of making the association of the discipline with his naughty deed.)

MEALTIME

Mealtime should be a peaceful time for your puppy. Do not put his food and water bowls in a high-traffic area in the house. For example, give him his own little corner of the kitchen where he can eat undisturbed and where he will not be under foot. Do not allow small children or other family members to disturb the pup when he is eating.

DID YOU KNOW?

If you have other pets in the home and/or interact often with the pets of friends and other family members, your pup will respond to those pets in much the same manner as you do. It is only when you show fear of or resentment toward another animal that he will act fearful or unfriendly.

Other times of excitement, such as family parties, etc., can be fun for the puppy providing he can view the activities from the security of his designated area. He is not underfoot and he is not being fed all sorts of titbits that will probably cause him stomach distress, yet he still feels a part of the fun.

SCHEDULE

A puppy should be taken to his relief area each time he is released from his designated area, after meals, after a play session, when he first awakens in the morning (at age eight weeks, this can mean 5 a.m.!). The puppy will indicate that

Crates are available in many sizes and made from a variety of materials. Get an appropriately sized crate for your Afghan and make it comfortable with bedding and a toy.

he's ready 'to go' by circling or sniffing busily—do not misinterpret these signs. For a puppy less than ten weeks of age, a routine of taking him out every hour is necessary. As the puppy grows, he will be able to wait for longer periods of time.

Keep trips to his relief area short. Stay no more than five or six minutes and then return to the house. If he goes during that time, praise him lavishly and take him indoors immediately.

DID YOU KNOW?

HOW MANY TIMES A DAY?

AGE	RELIEF TRIPS
To 14 weeks	10
14–22 weeks	8
22–32 weeks	6
Adulthood (dog stops growing)	4

These are estimates, of course, but they are a guide to the MINIMUM opportunities a dog should have each day to relieve itself.

If he does not, but he has an accident when you go back indoors, pick him up immediately, say 'No! No!' and return to his relief area. Wait a few minutes, then return to the house again. Never hit a puppy or rub his face in urine or excrement when he has had an accident!

Once indoors, put the puppy in his crate until you have had time to clean up his accident. Then release him to the family area and watch him more closely than before. Chances are, his accident was a result of your not picking up his signal or waiting too long before offering him the opportunity to relieve himself. Never hold a grudge against the puppy for accidents.

Let the puppy learn that going outdoors means it is time to relieve himself, not play. Once trained, he will be able to play indoors and out and still differentiate between the times for play versus the times for relief.

Help him develop regular hours for naps, being alone, playing by himself and just resting, all in his crate. Encourage him to entertain himself whilst you are busy with your activities. Each time you put a puppy in his own area, use the same command, whatever suits best. Soon, he will run to his crate or special area when he hears you say those words.

Crate training provides safety for you, the puppy and the home. It also provides the puppy with a feeling of security, and that helps the puppy achieve self-confidence and clean habits.

Remember that one of the primary ingredients in housetraining your puppy is control. Regardless of your lifestyle, there will always be occasions when you will need to have a place where your dog can stay and be happy and safe. Crate training is the answer for now and in the future.

In conclusion, a few key elements are really all you need for a successful house training method—consistency, frequency, praise, control and supervision. By following these procedures with a normal, healthy puppy, you and the puppy will soon be past the stage of 'accidents' and ready to move on to a full and rewarding life together.

ROLES OF DISCIPLINE, REWARD AND PUNISHMENT

Discipline, training one to act in accordance with rules, brings order to life. It is as simple as that. Without discipline, particularly in a group society, chaos reigns supreme and the group

HOUSEBREAKING TIP

Most of all, be consistent. Always take your dog to the same location, always use the same command, and always have him on lead when he is in his relief area, unless a fenced-in garden is available.

By following the Success Method, your puppy will be completely housetrained by the time his muscle and brain development reach maturity. Keep in mind that small breeds usually mature faster than large breeds, but all puppies should be trained by six months of age.

will eventually perish. Humans and canines are social animals and need some form of discipline in order to function effectively. They must procure food, protect their home base and their young and reproduce to keep the species going.

If there were no discipline in the lives of social animals, they would eventually die from starvation and/or predation by other stronger animals.

In the case of

THE SUCCESS METHOD

Success that comes by luck is usually short lived. Success that comes by well-thought-out proven methods is often more easily achieved and permanent. This is the Success Method. It is designed to give you, the puppy owner, a simple yet proven way to help your puppy develop clean living habits and a feeling of security in his new environment.

THE SUCCESS METHOD

1 Tell the puppy 'Crate time!' and place him in the crate with a small treat (a piece of cheese or half of a biscuit). Let him stay in the crate for five minutes while you are in the same room. Then release him and praise lavishly. Never release him when he is fussing. Wait until he is quiet before you let him out.

2 Repeat Step 1 several times a day.

3 The next day, place the puppy in the crate as before. Let him stay there for ten minutes. Do this several times.

4 Continue building time in five-minute increments until the puppy

stays in his crate for 30 minutes with you in the room. Always take him to his relief area after prolonged periods in his crate.

5 Now go back to Step 1 and let the puppy stay in his crate for five minutes, this time while you are out of the room.

6 Once again, build crate time in five-minute increments with you out of the room. When the puppy will stay willingly in his crate (he may even fall asleep!) for 30 minutes with you out of the room, he will be ready to stay in it for several hours at a time.

6 Steps to Successful Crate Training

The crate becomes your Afghan's home-away-from-home while travelling.

DID YOU KNOW?

By providing sleeping and resting quarters that fit the dog, and offering frequent opportunities to relieve himself outside his quarters, the puppy quickly learns that the outdoors (or the newspaper if you are training him to paper) is the place to go when he needs to urinate or defecate. It also reinforces his innate desire to keep his sleeping quarters clean. This, in turn, helps develop the muscle control that will eventually produce a dog with clean living habits.

domestic canines, dogs need discipline in their lives in order to understand how their pack (you and other family members) functions and how they must act in order to survive.

A large humane society in a highly populated area recently surveyed dog owners regarding their satisfaction with their relationships with their dogs. People who had trained their dogs were 75% more satisfied with their pets than those who had never trained their dogs.

Dr Edward Thorndike, a

DID YOU KNOW?

The puppy should also have regular play and exercise sessions when he is with you or a family member. Exercise for a very young puppy can

consist of a short walk around the house or garden. Playing can include fetching games with a large ball or a special raggy. (All puppies teethe and need soft things upon which to chew.) Remember to restrict play periods to indoors within his living area (the family room, for example) until he is completely housetrained.

psychologist, established *Thorndike's Theory of Learning*, which states that a behaviour that results in a pleasant event tends to be repeated. A behaviour that results in an unpleasant event tends not to be repeated. It is this theory on which training methods are

based today. For example, if you manipulate a dog to perform a specific behaviour and reward him for doing it, he is likely to

PRACTICE MAKES PERFECT

• Have training lessons with your dog every day in several short segments—three to five times a day for a few minutes at a time is ideal.

• Do not have long practice sessions. The dog will become easily bored.
• Never practise when you are tired, ill, worried or in an otherwise negative mood. This will transmit to the dog and may have an adverse effect on its performance.
  Think fun, short and above all POSITIVE! End each session on a high note, rather than a failed exercise, and make sure to give a lot of praise. Enjoy the training and help your dog enjoy it, too.

do it again because he enjoyed the end result.

Occasionally, punishment, a penalty inflicted for an offence, is necessary. The best type of punishment often comes from an outside source. For example, a child is told not to touch the stove because he may get burned. He disobeys and touches the stove. In doing so, he receives a burn. From that time on, he respects the heat of the stove and avoids contact with it. Therefore, a behaviour that results in an unpleasant event tends not to be repeated.

A good example of a dog learning the hard way is the dog who chases the house cat. He is told many times to leave the cat alone, yet he persists in teasing the cat. Then, one day he begins chasing the cat but the cat turns and swipes a claw across the dog's face, leaving him with a painful gash on his nose. The final result is that the dog stops chasing the cat.

TRAINING EQUIPMENT

COLLAR AND LEAD

For an Afghan Hound the collar and lead that you use for training must be one with which you are easily able to work, not too heavy for the dog and perfectly safe.

'Nice to meet you!' It's not too difficult for different pets to get along in the same household, as long as they are given the opportunity to get acquainted.

TREATS

Have a bag of treats on hand. Something nutritious and easy to swallow works best. Use a soft treat, a chunk of cheese or a piece of cooked chicken rather than a dry biscuit. By the time the dog has finished chewing a dry treat, he will forget why he is being rewarded in the first place! Using food rewards will not teach a dog to beg at the table—the only way to teach a dog to beg at the table is to give him food from the table. In training, rewarding the dog with a food treat will help him associate praise and the treats with learning new behaviours that obviously please his owner.

TRAINING BEGINS: ASK THE DOG A QUESTION

In order to teach your dog anything, you must first get his attention. After all, he cannot learn anything if he is looking away from you with his mind on something else.

To get his attention, ask him, 'School?' and immediately walk over to him and give him a treat as you tell him 'Good dog.' Wait a minute or two and repeat the routine, this time with a treat in your hand as you approach within a foot of the dog. Do not go directly to him, but stop about a foot short of him and hold out the treat as you ask, 'School?' He will see you approaching with a treat in your hand and most likely begin walking toward you. As you meet, give him the treat and praise again.

TRAINING TIP

Your dog is actually training you at the same time you are training him. Dogs do things to get attention.

They usually repeat whatever succeeds in getting your attention.

The third time, ask the question, have a treat in your hand and walk only a short distance toward the dog so that he must walk almost all the way to you. As he reaches you, give him the treat and praise again.

By this time, the dog will probably be getting the idea that if he pays attention to you, especially when you ask that question, it will pay off in treats and enjoyable activities for him. In other words, he learns that 'School' means doing things with you that result in treats and positive attention for him.

Remember that the dog does not understand your verbal language, he only recognises sounds. Your question translates to a series of sounds for him, and those sounds become the signal to go to you and pay attention; if he does, he will get to interact with you plus receive treats and praise.

THE BASIC COMMANDS

TEACHING SIT

Now that you have the dog's attention, attach his lead and hold it in your left hand and a food treat in your right. Place your food hand at the dog's nose and let him lick the treat but not take it from you. Say 'Sit' and slowly raise your food hand from in front of the dog's nose

Treats are wonderful motivators when teaching new commands. You won't have trouble holding your Afghan's attention if you show him a tasty reward.

These two well-groomed windhounds are enjoying a walk on lead with their owner.

TRAINING TIP

Stand up straight and authoritatively when giving your dog commands. Do not issue commands when lying on the floor or lying on your back on the sofa. If you are on your hands and knees when you give a command, your dog will think you are positioning yourself to play.

The food treat should be visible to the dog before you start the exercise.

up over his head so that he is looking at the ceiling. As he bends his head upward, he will have to bend his knees to maintain his balance. As he bends his knees, he will assume a sit position. At that point, release the food treat and praise lavishly with comments such as 'Good dog! Good sit!', etc. Remember to always praise enthusiastically, because dogs relish verbal praise from their owners and feel so proud of themselves whenever they accomplish a behaviour.

You will not use food forever in getting the dog to obey your commands. Food is only used to teach new behaviours, and once the dog knows what you want when you give a specific command, you will wean him off the food treats but still maintain the verbal praise. After all, you will always have your voice with you, and there will be many times when you have no food rewards but expect the dog to obey.

TEACHING DOWN

Teaching the down exercise is easy when you understand how the dog perceives the down position, and it is very difficult when you do not. Dogs perceive the down position as a submissive one, therefore teaching the down exercise using a forceful method can make the dog develop such a fear of the down that he either runs away when you say 'Down' or he attempts to snap at the person who tries to force him down. Afghans *never* feel submissive.

Have the dog sit close alongside your left leg, facing in the same direction as you are. Hold the lead in your left hand and a food treat in your right. Now place your left hand lightly on the top of the dog's shoulders where they meet above the spinal cord. Do not push down on the dog's shoulders; simply rest your left hand there so you can guide the dog to lie down close to your left leg rather than to swing away from your side when he drops.

Now place the food hand at the dog's nose, say 'Down' very softly (almost a whisper), and slowly lower the food hand to the dog's front feet. When the food hand reaches the floor, begin moving it forward along the floor in front of the dog. Keep talking softly to the dog, saying things like, 'Do you want this treat? You can do this, good dog.' Your reassuring tone of voice will help calm the dog as he tries to follow the food hand in order to get the treat.

When the dog's elbows touch the floor, release the food and praise softly. Try to get the dog to maintain that down position for several seconds

TRAINING TIP

A dog in jeopardy never lies down. He stays alert on his feet because instinct tells him that he may have

to run away or fight for his survival. Therefore, if a dog feels threatened or anxious, he will not lie down. Consequently, it is important to have the dog calm and relaxed as he learns the down exercise.

The SIT command is a basic command that is easy to teach.

before you let him sit up again. The goal here is to get the dog to settle down and not feel threatened in the down position.

TEACHING STAY

It is easy to teach the dog to stay in either a sit or a down position. Again, we use food and praise during the teaching process as we help the dog to understand exactly what it is that we are expecting him to do.

To teach the sit/stay, start with the dog sitting on your left side as before and hold the lead

THE GOLDEN RULE

The golden rule of dog training is simple. For each 'question' (command), there is only one

correct answer (reaction). One command = one reaction. Keep practising the command until the dog reacts correctly without hesitating. Be repetitive but not monotonous. Dogs get bored just as people do!

in your left hand. Have a food treat in your right hand and place your food hand at the dog's nose. Say 'Stay' and step out on your right foot to stand directly in front of the dog, toe to toe, as he licks and nibbles the treat. Be sure to keep his head facing upward to maintain the sit position. Count to five and then swing around to stand next to the dog again with him on your left. As soon as you get back to the original position, release the food and praise lavishly.

To teach the down/stay, do the down as previously described. As soon as the dog lies down, say 'Stay' and step out on your right foot just as you did in the sit/stay. Count to five and then return to stand beside the dog with him on your left side. Release the treat and praise as always.

Within a week or ten days, you can begin to add a bit of distance between you and your dog when you leave him. When you do, use your left hand open with the palm facing the dog as a stay signal, much the same as

TRAINING TIP

Play fetch games with your puppy in an enclosed area where he can retrieve his toy and bring it back to you. Always use a toy or object designated just for this purpose. Never use a shoe, stocking or other item he may later confuse with those in your wardrobe or underneath your chair.

the hand signal a constable uses to stop traffic at an intersection. Hold the food treat in your right hand as before, but this time the food is not touching the dog's nose. He will watch the food hand and quickly learn that he is going to get that treat as soon as you return to his side.

When you can stand 1 metre away from your dog for 30 seconds, you can then begin building time and distance in both stays. Eventually, the dog can be expected to remain in the stay position for prolonged periods of time until you return to him or call him to you. Always praise lavishly when he stays.

TEACHING COME

If you make teaching 'come' a positive experience, you should never have a 'student' that does not love the game or that fails to come when called. The secret, it seems, is never to teach the word 'come.'

At times when an owner most wants his dog to come when called, the owner is likely

The stay command should be taught initially with the dog on lead. Trainers often use the hand signal shown here along with the verbal command.

111

TRAINING TIP

Dogs will do anything for your attention. If you reward the dog when he is calm and resting, you will develop a well-mannered dog. If, on

the other hand, you greet your dog excitedly and encourage him to wrestle and roughhouse with you, the dog will greet you the same way and you will have a hyper dog on your hands.

to be upset or anxious and he allows these feelings to come through in the tone of his voice when he calls his dog. Hearing that desperation in his owner's voice, the dog fears the results of going to him and therefore either disobeys outright or runs in the opposite direction. The secret, therefore, is to teach the dog a game and, when you want him to come to you, simply

play the game. It is practically a no-fail solution though nothing is guaranteed with an Afghan!

To begin, have several members of your family take a few food treats and each go into a different room in the house. Take turns calling the dog, and each person should celebrate the dog's finding him with a treat and lots of happy praise. When a person calls the dog, he is actually inviting the dog to find him and get a treat as a reward for 'winning.'

A few turns of the 'Where are you?' game and the dog will understand that everyone is playing the game and that each person has a big celebration awaiting his success at locating them. Once he learns to love the game, simply calling out 'Where are you?' should bring him running from wherever he is when he hears that all-important question.

The come command is recognised as one of the most important things to teach a dog, but there are trainers who work with thousands of dogs and never teach the actual word 'Come.' Yet these dogs will race to respond to a person who uses the dog's name followed by 'Where are you?' For example, a woman has a 12-year-old companion dog who went blind, but who never fails to locate her owner when

TRAINING TIP

Never call your dog to come to you for a correction or scold him when he reaches you. That is the quickest way to turn a 'Come' command into 'Go away fast!' Dogs think only in the present tense, and your dog will connect the scolding with coming to you, not with the misbehaviour of a few moments earlier.

TRAINING TIP

Occasionally, a dog and owner who have not attended formal classes have been able to earn entry-level

titles by obtaining competition rules and regulations from a local kennel club and practising on their own to a degree of perfection. Obtaining the higher level titles, however, almost always requires extensive training under the tutelage of experienced instructors. In addition, the more difficult levels require more specialised equipment whereas the lower levels do not.

asked, 'Where are you?'

Children particularly love to play this game with their dogs. Children can hide in smaller places like a shower or bath, behind a bed or under a table. The dog needs to work a little bit harder to find these hiding places, but when he does he loves to celebrate with a treat and a tussle with a favourite youngster.

TEACHING HEEL

Heeling means that the dog walks beside the owner without pulling. It takes time and patience on the owner's part to succeed at teaching the dog that he (the owner) will not proceed unless the dog is walking calmly beside him. Pulling out ahead on the lead is definitely not acceptable.

Begin with holding the lead in your left hand as the dog sits beside your left leg. Move the loop end of the lead to your

TRAINING TIP

If you begin teaching the heel by taking long walks and letting the dog pull you along, he misinterprets this action as an acceptable form of

taking a walk. When you pull back on the lead to counteract his pulling, he reads that tug as a signal to pull even harder!

verbally, but do not touch the dog. Hesitate a moment and begin again with 'Heel,' taking three steps and stopping, at which point the dog is told to sit again.

Your goal here is to have the dog walk those three steps without pulling on the lead. When he will walk calmly beside you for three steps without pulling, increase the number of steps you take to five. When he will walk politely beside you whilst you take five steps, you can increase the length of your walk to ten steps. Keep increasing the length of your stroll until the dog will walk quietly beside you without pulling as long as you want him to heel. When you stop heeling, indicate to the dog that the exercise is over by verbally praising as you pet him and say 'OK, good dog.' The 'OK' is used as a release word meaning

TRAINING TIP

When calling the dog, do not say 'Come.' Say things like, 'Rover, where are you? See if you can find me! I have a biscuit for you!' Keep up a constant line of chatter with coaxing sounds and frequent questions such as, 'Where are you?' The dog will learn to follow the sound of your voice to locate you and receive his reward.

right hand but keep your left hand short on the lead so it keeps the dog in close next to you.

Say 'Heel' and step forward on your left foot. Keep the dog close to you and take three steps. Stop and have the dog sit next to you in what we now call the 'heel position.' Praise

that the exercise is finished and the dog is free to relax.

If you are dealing with a dog who insists on pulling you around, simply 'put on your brakes' and stand your ground until the dog realises that the two of you are not going anywhere until he is beside you and moving at your pace, not his. It may take some time just standing there to convince the dog that you are the leader and you will be the one to decide on the direction and speed of your travel.

Each time the dog looks up at you or slows down to give a slack lead between the two of you, quietly praise him and say, 'Good heel. Good dog.' Eventually, the dog will begin to respond and soon he will be walking politely beside you without pulling on the lead. At first, the training sessions should be kept short and very positive; soon the dog will be able to walk nicely with you for increasingly longer distances. Remember also to give the dog free time and the opportunity to

TRAINING TIP

Teach your dog to HEEL in an enclosed area. Once you think the dog will obey reliably and you want

to attempt advanced obedience exercises such as off-lead heeling, test him in a fenced-in area so he cannot run away.

run and play when you have finished heel practice.

WEANING OFF FOOD IN TRAINING

Food is used in training new behaviours. Once the dog understands what behaviour goes with a specific command, it is time to start weaning him off the food treats. At first, give a treat after each exercise. Then, start to give a treat only after

TRAINING TIP

If you are walking your dog and he suddenly stops and looks straight into your eyes, ignore him. Pull the leash and lead him into the direction you want to walk.

TRAINING TIP

Dogs are the most honourable animals in existence. They consider another species (humans) as their own. They interface with you. You are their leader. Puppies perceive children to be on their level; their actions around small children are different from their behaviour around their adult masters.

every other exercise. Mix up the times when you offer a food reward and the times when you only offer praise so that the dog will never know when he is going to receive both food and praise and when he is going to receive only praise. This is called a variable ratio reward system and it proves successful because there is always the chance that the owner will produce a treat, so the dog never stops trying for that reward. No matter what, ALWAYS give verbal praise.

OBEDIENCE CLASSES
It is a good idea to enrol in an obedience class if one is available in your area. If yours is a show dog, ringcraft classes would be more appropriate. Many areas have dog clubs that offer basic obedience training as well as preparatory classes for obedience competition.

The combination of basic training, socialisation and possibly ringcraft classes make a well-behaved dog who will stand politely for a judge's evaluation.

There are also local dog trainers who offer similar classes.

At obedience trials, dogs can earn titles at various levels of competition. The beginning levels of competition include basic behaviours such as sit, down, heel, etc. The more advanced levels of competition include jumping, retrieving, scent discrimination and signal work. The advanced levels require a dog and owner to put a lot of time and effort into their training and the titles that can be earned at these levels of competition are very prestigious.

OTHER ACTIVITIES FOR LIFE
Whether a dog is trained in the structured environment of a class or alone with his owner at home, there are many activities that can bring fun and rewards to both owner and dog once they have mastered basic control.

THINK BEFORE YOU BARK!

Dogs are sensitive to their master's moods and emotions. Use your voice wisely when communicating with your dog. Never raise your voice at your dog unless you are angry and trying to correct him. 'Barking' at your dog can become as meaningless as 'dogspeak' is to you. Think before you bark!

DID YOU KNOW?

Although many of the sighthound breeds, including the Afghan Hound,

compete and fare well in coursing, the most famous of all coursing events is The Waterloo Cup for Greyhounds, held in February at the great Altcar Estate in Lancashire. Founded by Earl Sefton in 1836, coinciding with Aintree's Grand National Steeple-chase, this annual event is still considered the most coveted award for any Greyhound.

Teaching the dog to help out around the home, in the garden or on the farm provides great satisfaction to both dog and owner. In addition, the dog's help makes life a little easier for his owner and raises his stature as a valued companion to his family. It helps give the dog a purpose by occupying his mind and providing an outlet for his energy.

If you are interested in

Engage your speedy Afghan Hound in a sighthound sport. It will be a most exciting endeavour for both of you.

participating in organised competition with your Afghan Hound, there are activities other than obedience in which you and your dog can become involved.

RACING, LURE COURSING AND COURSING

Lure coursing is an exciting and healthy activity that is a natural for Afghan Hounds. In lure coursing, dogs chase a lure, which of course cannot change direction as a live quarry can but still provides an opportunity for your Afghan Hound to follow its instinctual need to chase a quarry.

AGILITY

Agility is a popular and enjoyable sport where dogs run through an obstacle course that includes various jumps, tunnels and other exercises to test the dog's speed and coordination. The owners run through the course beside their dogs to give commands and to guide them through the course. Although competitive, the focus is on fun—it's fun to do, fun to watch, and great exercise.

Dogs suffer many of the same physical illnesses as people. They might even share many of the same psychological problems. Since people usually know more about human diseases than canine maladies, many of the terms used in this chapter will be familiar but not necessarily those used by veterinary surgeons. We will use the term *x-ray*, instead of the more acceptable term *radiograph*. We will also use the familiar term *symptoms* even though dogs don't have symptoms, which are verbal descriptions of the patient's feelings; dogs have *clinical signs*. Since dogs can't speak, we have to look for clinical signs...but we still use the term *symptoms* in this book.

As a general rule, medicine is *practised*. That term is not arbitrary. Medicine is a constantly changing art as we learn more and more about genetics, electronic aids (like CAT scans) and daily laboratory advances. There are many dog maladies, like canine hip dysplasia, which are not universally treated in the same manner. Some veterinary surgeons opt for surgery more often than others do.

SELECTING A VETERINARY SURGEON

Your selection of a veterinary surgeon should not be based upon personality (as most are) but upon their convenience to your home. You require a veterinary surgeon who is close because you might have emergencies or need to make multiple visits for treatments. You require a vet who has services that you might require such as tattooing and grooming facilities, as well as sophisticated pet supplies and a good reputation for ability and responsiveness. There is nothing more frustrating than having to wait a day or more to

Before you buy a dog, meet and interview the veterinary surgeons in your area. Take everything into consideration; discuss background, specialities, fees, emergency policies, etc.

get a response from your veterinary surgeon.

All veterinary surgeons are licensed and their diplomas and/or certificates should be displayed in their waiting rooms. There are, however, many veterinary specialities that usually require further studies and internships. There are specialists in heart problems (veterinary cardiologists), skin problems (veterinary dermatologists), teeth and gum problems (veterinary dentists), eye problems (veterinary ophthalmologists), x-rays (veterinary radiologists), and surgeons who have specialities in bones, muscles or other organs. Most veterinary surgeons do routine surgery such as neutering, stitching up wounds and docking tails for those breeds in which such is required for show purposes. When the problem affecting your dog is serious, it is not unusual or impudent to get another medical opinion, although in Britain you are obliged to advise the vets concerned about this. You might also want to compare costs amongst several veterinary surgeons. Sophisticated health care and veterinary services can be very costly. Don't be bashful about discussing these costs with your veterinary surgeon or his (her) staff. Important decisions are often based upon financial considerations.

DID YOU KNOW?

The myth that dogs need extra fat in their diets can be harmful. Should your vet recommend extra fat, use safflower oil instead of animal oils. Safflower oil has been shown to be less likely to cause allergic reactions.

PREVENTATIVE MEDICINE

It is much easier, less costly and more effective to practise preventative medicine than to fight bouts of illness and disease. Properly bred puppies come from parents who were selected based upon their genetic disease profile. Their mothers should have been vaccinated, free of all internal and external parasites, and properly nourished. For these reasons, a visit to the veterinary surgeon who cared for the dam (mother) is recommended. The dam can pass on disease resistance to her puppies, which can last for eight to ten weeks. She can

DID YOU KNOW?

Vaccinations help prevent your new puppy from contracting diseases, but they do not cure them. Proper nutrition as well as parasite control keep your dog healthy and less susceptible to many dangerous diseases. Remember that your dog depends on you to ensure his well being.

Your veterinary surgeon should teach you how to administer medicine to your Afghan should it become necessary.

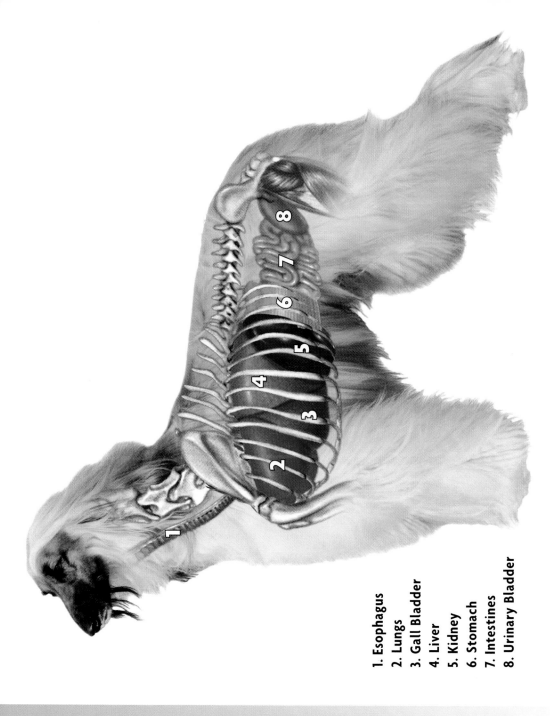

1. Esophagus
2. Lungs
3. Gall Bladder
4. Liver
5. Kidney
6. Stomach
7. Intestines
8. Urinary Bladder

Internal Organs of the Afghan Hound

also pass on parasites and many infections. That's why you should visit the veterinary surgeon who cared for the dam.

WEANING TO FIVE MONTHS OLD

Puppies should be weaned by the time they are about two months old. A puppy that remains for at least eight weeks with its mother and littermates usually adapts better to other dogs and people later in its life.

Some new owners have their puppy examined by a veterinary surgeon immediately, which is a good idea. Vaccination programmes usually begin when the puppy is very young.

The puppy will have its teeth examined and have its skeletal conformation and general health checked prior to certification by the veterinary surgeon. Puppies in certain breeds have problems with

their kneecaps, eye cataracts and other eye problems, heart murmurs and undescended testicles. They may also have personality problems and your veterinary surgeon might have training in temperament evaluation.

VACCINATION SCHEDULING

Most vaccinations are given by injection and should only be done by a veterinary surgeon. Both he and you should keep a record of the date of the injection, the identification of the vaccine and the amount given. Some vets give a first vaccination at eight weeks, but most dog breeders prefer the course not to commence until about ten weeks because of negating any antibodies passed on by the dam. The vaccination scheduling is usually based on a 15-day cycle. You must take your vet's advice as to when to vaccinate as this may differ according to the vaccine used. Most vaccinations immunize your puppy against viruses.

The usual vaccines contain immunizing doses of several

HEALTH AND VACCINATION SCHEDULE

AGE IN WEEKS:	6TH	8TH	10TH	12TH	14TH	16TH	20-24TH	1 YR
Worm Control	✔	✔	✔	✔	✔	✔	✔	
Neutering								✔
Heartworm*		✔		✔		✔	✔	
Parvovirus	✔		✔		✔		✔	✔
Distemper		✔		✔		✔		✔
Hepatitis		✔		✔		✔		✔
Leptospirosis								✔
Parainfluenza	✔		✔		✔			✔
Dental Examination		✔					✔	✔
Complete Physical		✔					✔	✔
Coronavirus				✔			✔	✔
Kennel Cough	✔							
Hip Dysplasia								✔
Rabies*							✔	

Vaccinations are not instantly effective. It takes about two weeks for the dog's immunization system to develop antibodies. Most vaccinations require annual booster shots. Your veterinary surgeon should guide you in this regard.
*Not applicable in the United Kingdom

different viruses such as distemper, parvovirus, parainfluenza and hepatitis. There are other vaccines available when the puppy is at risk. You should rely upon professional advice. This is especially true for the booster-shot programme. Most vaccination programmes require a booster when the puppy is a year old and once a year thereafter. In some cases, circumstances may require more or less frequent immunizations. Kennel cough, more formally known as tracheobronchitis, is treated with a vaccine that is sprayed into the dog's nostrils. Kennel cough is usually included in routine vaccination, but this is often not so effective as for other major diseases.

FIVE MONTHS TO ONE YEAR OF AGE
Unless you intend to breed or show your dog, neutering the puppy at six months of age is recommended. Discuss this with your veterinary surgeon; most professionals advise neutering the puppy. Neutering has proven to be extremely beneficial to both male and female puppies. Besides eliminating the possibility of pregnancy, it inhibits (but does not prevent) breast cancer in bitches and prostate cancer in male dogs. Under no circumstances should a

bitch be spayed prior to her first season.

Your veterinary surgeon should provide your puppy with a thorough dental evaluation at six months of age, ascertaining whether all the permanent teeth have erupted properly. A home dental care regimen should be initiated at six months, including brushing weekly and providing good dental devices (such as nylon bones). Regular dental care promotes healthy teeth, fresh breath and a longer life.

ONE TO SEVEN YEARS

Once a year, your grown dog should visit the vet for an examination and vaccination boosters. Some vets recommend blood tests, thyroid level check and dental evaluation to accompany these annual visits. A thorough clinical evaluation by the vet can provide critical background information for your dog. Blood tests are often performed at one year of age, and dental examinations around the third or fourth birthday. In the

DISEASE REFERENCE CHART

	What is it?	What causes it?	Symptoms
Leptospirosis	Severe disease that affects the internal organs; can be spread to people.	A bacterium, which is often carried by rodents, that enters through mucous membranes and spreads quickly throughout the body.	Range from fever, vomiting and loss of appetite in less severe cases to shock, irreversible kidney damage and possibly death in most severe cases.
Rabies	Potentially deadly virus that infects warm-blooded mammals. Not seen in United Kingdom.	Bite from a carrier of the virus, mainly wild animals.	1st stage: dog exhibits change in behaviour, fear. 2nd stage: dog's behaviour becomes more aggressive. 3rd stage: loss of coordination, trouble with bodily functions.
Parvovirus	Highly contagious virus, potentially deadly.	Ingestion of the virus, which is usually spread through the faeces of infected dogs.	Most common: severe diarrhoea. Also vomiting, fatigue, lack of appetite.
Kennel cough	Contagious respiratory infection.	Combination of types of bacteria and virus. Most common: *Bordetella bronchiseptica* bacteria and parainfluenza virus.	Chronic cough.
Distemper	Disease primarily affecting respiratory and nervous system.	Virus that is related to the human measles virus.	Mild symptoms such as fever, lack of appetite and mucous secretion progress to evidence of brain damage, 'hard pad.'
Hepatitis	Virus primarily affecting the liver.	Canine adenovirus type I (CAV-1). Enters system when dog breathes in particles.	Lesser symptoms include listlessness, diarrhoea, vomiting. More severe symptoms include 'blue-eye' (clumps of virus in eye).
Coronavirus	Virus resulting in digestive problems.	Virus is spread through infected dog's faeces.	Stomach upset evidenced by lack of appetite, vomiting, diarrhoea.

long run, quality preventative care for your pet can save money, teeth and lives.

SKIN PROBLEMS IN AFGHAN HOUNDS

Veterinary surgeons are consulted by dog owners for skin problems more than any other group of diseases or maladies. Dogs' skin is

DID YOU KNOW?

Vaccines do not work all the time. Sometimes dogs are allergic to them and many times the antibodies, which are supposed to be stimulated by the vaccine, just are not produced. You should keep your

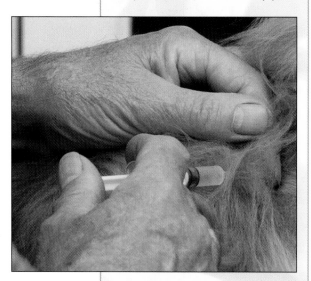

dog in the veterinary clinic for an hour after it is vaccinated to be sure there are no allergic reactions.

DID YOU KNOW?

Cases of hyperactive adrenal glands (Cushing's disease) have been traced to the drinking of highly chlorinated water. Aerate or age your dog's drinking water before offering it.

almost as sensitive as human skin and both suffer almost the same ailments (though the occurrence of acne in dogs is rare!). For this reason, veterinary dermatology has developed into a speciality practised by many veterinary surgeons.

Since many skin problems have visual symptoms that are almost identical, it requires the skill of an experienced veterinary dermatologist to identify and cure many of the more severe skin disorders. Pet shops sell many

'P' STANDS FOR PROBLEM

Urinary tract disease is a serious condition that requires immediate medical attention. Symptoms include urinating in inappropriate places or the need to urinate frequently in small amounts. Urinary tract disease is most effectively treated with antibiotics. To help promote good urinary tract health, owners must always be sure that a constant supply of fresh water is available to their pets.

PARVO FOR THE COURSE

Canine parvovirus is a highly contagious disease that attacks puppies and older dogs. Spread through contact with infected faeces, parvovirus causes bloody diarrhoea, vomiting, heart damage, dehydration, shock and death. To prevent this tragedy, have your puppy begin his series of vaccinations at six to eight weeks. Be aware that the virus is easily spread and is carried on a dog's hair and feet, water bowls and other objects, as well as people's shoes and clothing.

treatments for skin problems but most of the treatments are directed at symptoms and not the underlying problem(s). If your dog is suffering from a skin disorder, you should seek professional assistance as quickly as possible. As with all diseases, the earlier a problem is identified and treated, the more successful is the cure.

HEREDITARY SKIN DISORDERS

Veterinary dermatologists are currently researching a number of skin disorders that are believed to have a hereditary basis. These inherited diseases are transmitted by both parents, who appear (phenotypically) normal but have a recessive gene for the disease, meaning that they carry, but are not affected by, the disease. These diseases pose serious problems to breeders because in some instances there is no method of identifying carriers. Often the secondary diseases associated with these skin conditions are even more debilitating than the skin disorder, including cancers and respiratory problems; others can be lethal.

Amongst the known hereditary skin disorders, for which the

DID YOU KNOW?

Not every dog's ears are the same. Ears that are open to the air are healthier than ears with poor air circulation. Sometimes a dog can

have two differently shaped ears. You should not probe inside your dog's ears. Only clean that which is accessible with a soft cotton wipe.

DID YOU KNOW?

A dental examination is in order when the dog is between six months and one year of age so any permanent teeth that have erupted incorrectly can be corrected. It is important to begin a brushing routine, preferably using a two-sided brushing technique, whereby both sides of the tooth are brushed at the same time. Durable nylon and safe edible chews should be a part of your puppy's arsenal for good health, good teeth and pleasant

breath. The vast majority of dogs three to four years old and older has diseases of the gums from lack of dental attention. Using the various types of dental chews can be very effective in controlling dental plaque.

mode of inheritance is known, are acrodermatitis, cutaneous asthenia (Ehlers-Danlos syndrome), sebaceous adenitis, cyclic hematopoiesis, dermatomyositis, IgA deficiency, colour dilution alopecia and nodular dermatofibrosis. Some of these disorders are limited to one or two breeds and others affect a large number of breeds. All inherited diseases must be diagnosed and treated by a veterinary specialist.

PARASITE BITES

Many of us are allergic to insect bites. The bites itch, erupt and may even become infected. Dogs have the same reaction to fleas, ticks and/or mites. When an insect lands on you, you have the chance to whisk it away with your hand. Unfortunately, when your dog is bitten by a flea, tick or mite, it can only scratch it away or bite it. By the time the dog has been bitten, the parasite has done some of its damage. It may also have laid eggs to cause further problems in the near future. The itching from parasite bites is probably due to the saliva injected into the site when the parasite sucks the dog's blood.

AUTO-IMMUNE SKIN CONDITIONS

Auto-immune skin conditions are commonly referred to as being allergic to yourself, whilst allergies are usually inflammatory reactions to an outside stimulus.

Combing your Afghan's hair gives you the opportunity to inspect its body and coat for abnormalities and parasites.

Auto-immune diseases cause serious damage to the tissues that are involved.

The best known auto-immune disease is lupus, which affects people as well as dogs. The symptoms are variable and may affect the kidneys, bones, blood chemistry and skin. It can be fatal to both dogs and humans, though it is not thought to be transmissible. It is usually successfully treated with cortisone, prednisone or similar corticosteroid, but extensive use of these drugs can have harmful side effects.

AIRBORNE ALLERGIES

An interesting allergy is pollen allergy. Humans have hay fever, rose fever and other fevers with which they suffer during the pollinating season. Many dogs suffer the same allergies. When

DID YOU KNOW?

Chances are that you and your dog will have the same allergies. Your allergies are readily recognisable and usually easily treated. Your dog's allergies may be masked.

Some eye problems are treated with prescription eye drops that you administer at home.

FOOD PROBLEMS

FOOD ALLERGIES

Dogs are allergic to many foods that are best-sellers and highly recommended by breeders and veterinary surgeons. Changing the brand of food that you buy may not eliminate the problem if the element to which the dog is allergic is contained in the new brand.

Recognising a food allergy is difficult. Humans vomit or have rashes when they eat a food to which they are allergic. Dogs neither vomit nor (usually) develop a rash. They react in the same manner as they do to an airborne or flea allergy: they itch, scratch and bite, thus making the diagnosis extremely difficult. Whilst pollen allergies and parasite bites are usually seasonal,

the pollen count is high, your dog might suffer but don't expect him to sneeze and have a runny nose like humans do. Dogs react to pollen allergies the same way they react to fleas—they scratch and bite themselves.

Dogs, like humans, can be tested for allergens. Discuss the testing with your veterinary dermatologist.

Do not feed your Afghan 'people food.' First, it encourages the dog to beg for food when you are eating; second, food that you eat may be too fatty or spicy for the dog, upsetting the balance in his diet and possibly causing him stomach distress.

food allergies are year-round problems.

FOOD INTOLERANCE

Food intolerance is the inability of the dog to completely digest certain foods. Puppies that may have done very well on their mother's milk may not do well on cow's milk. The result of this food intolerance may be loose bowels, passing gas and stomach pains. These are the only obvious symptoms of food intolerance and that makes diagnosis difficult.

TREATING FOOD PROBLEMS

It is possible to handle food allergies and food intolerance yourself. Put your dog on a diet that it has never had. Obviously, if it has never eaten this new food, it can't have been allergic or intolerant of it. Start with a single ingredient that is not in the dog's diet at the present time. Ingredients like chopped beef or fish are common in dog's diets, so try something more exotic like rabbit, pheasant or even just vegetables. Keep the dog on this diet (with no additives) for a month. If the symptoms of food allergy or intolerance disappear, chances are your dog has a food allergy.

Don't think that the single ingredient cured the problem. You still must find a suitable diet and ascertain which ingredient in the old diet was objectionable. This is most easily done by adding

DID YOU KNOW?

Dogs who have been exposed to lawns sprayed with herbicides have double and triple the rate of malignant lymphoma. Town dogs are especially at risk, as they are

exposed to tailored lawns and gardens. Dogs perspire and absorb through their footpads. Be careful where your dog walks and always avoid any area that appears yellowed from chemical overspray.

ingredients to the new diet one at a time. Let the dog stay on the modified diet for a month before you add another ingredient. Eventually, you will determine the ingredient that caused the adverse reaction.

An alternative method is to carefully study the ingredients in the diet to which your dog is allergic or intolerant. Identify the main ingredient in this diet and eliminate the main ingredient by buying a different food that does not have that ingredient. Keep experimenting until the symptoms disappear after one month on the new diet.

A scanning electron micrograph (S. E. M.) of a dog flea, *Ctenocephalides canis.*

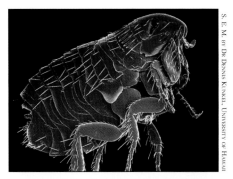

S. E. M. BY DR DENNIS KUNKEL, UNIVERSITY OF HAWAII

EXTERNAL PARASITES

Of all the problems to which dogs are prone, none is more well known and frustrating than fleas. Flea infestation is relatively simple to cure but difficult to prevent. Parasites that are harboured inside the body are a bit more difficult to eradicate but they are easier to control.

Magnified head of a dog flea, *Ctenocephalides canis.*

S. E. M. BY DR DENNIS KUNKEL, UNIVERSITY OF HAWAII

FLEAS

To control a flea infestation you have to understand the flea's life cycle. Fleas are often thought of as a summertime problem but centrally heated homes have changed the patterns and fleas can be found at any time of the year. The most effective method of flea control is a two-stage approach:

A male dog flea, *Ctenocephalides canis.*

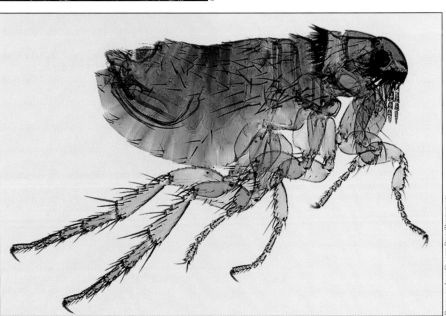

PHOTO BY JEAN CLAUDE REVY/PHOTOTAKE.

DID YOU KNOW?

Flea-killers are poisonous. You should not spray these toxic chemicals on areas of a dog's body that he licks, on his genitals or on his face. Flea killers taken internally are a better answer, but check with your vet in case internal therapy is not advised for your dog.

one stage to kill the adult fleas, and the other to control the development of pre-adult fleas. Unfortunately, no single active ingredient is effective against all stages of the life cycle.

LIFE CYCLE STAGES

During its life, a flea will pass through four life stages: egg, larva, pupa and adult. The adult stage is the most visible and irritating stage of the flea life cycle and this is why the majority of flea-control products concentrate on this stage. The fact is that adult fleas account for only 1% of the total flea population, and the other 99% exist in pre-adult stages, i.e. eggs, larvae and pupae. The pre-adult stages are barely visible to the naked eye.

THE LIFE CYCLE OF THE FLEA

Eggs are laid on the dog, usually in quantities of about 20 or 30, several times a day. The female adult flea must have a blood meal before each egg-laying session. When first laid, the eggs will cling to the dog's fur, as the eggs are still moist. However, they will quickly dry out and fall from the dog, especially if the dog moves around or scratches. Many eggs will fall off in the dog's favourite area or an area in which he spends a lot of time, such as his bed.

Once the eggs fall from the dog onto the carpet or furniture, they will hatch into larvae. This takes from one to ten days. Larvae are not particularly mobile, and will usually travel only a few inches from where they hatch. However, they do have a tendency to move

ILLUSTRATION COURTESY OF BAYER VITAL GMBH & CO. KG

A Look at Fleas

Fleas have been around for millions of years and have adapted to changing host animals. They are able to go through a complete life cycle in less than one month or they can extend their lives to almost two years by remaining as pupae or cocoons. They do not need blood or any other food for up to 20 months.

They have been measured as being able to jump 300,000 times and can jump 150 times their length in any direction including straight up. Those are just a few of the reasons why they are so successful in infesting a dog!

away from light and heavy traffic—under furniture and behind doors are common places to find high quantities of flea larvae.

The flea larvae feed on dead organic matter, including adult flea faeces, until they are ready to change into adult fleas. Fleas will usually remain as larvae for around seven days. After this period, the larvae will pupate into protective pupae. While inside the pupae, the larvae will undergo metamorphosis and change into adult fleas. This can take as little time as a few days, but the adult fleas can remain inside the pupae waiting to hatch for up to two years. The pupae are signalled to hatch by certain stimuli, such as physical pressure—the pupae's being stepped on, heat from an animal lying on the pupae or increased carbon dioxide levels and vibrations—indicating that a suitable host is available.

Once hatched, the adult flea must feed within a few days. Once the adult flea finds a host, it will not leave voluntarily. It only becomes dislodged by grooming or

En Garde: CATCHING FLEAS OFF GUARD

Consider the following ways to arm yourself against fleas:
• Add a small amount of pennyroyal or eucalyptus oil to your dog's bath. These natural remedies repel fleas.
• Supplement your dog's food with fresh garlic (minced or grated) and a hearty amount of brewer's yeast, both of which ward off fleas.
• Use a flea comb on your dog daily. Submerge fleas in a cup of bleach to kill them quickly.
• Confine the dog to only a few rooms to limit the spread of fleas in the home.
• Vacuum daily...and get all of the crevices! Dispose of the bag every few days until the problem is under control.
• Wash your dog's bedding daily. Cover cushions where your dog sleeps with towels, and wash the towels often.

DID YOU KNOW?

Never mix flea control products without first consulting your veterinary surgeon. Some products can become toxic when combined with others and can cause serious or fatal consequences.

the host animal's scratching. The adult flea will remain on the host for the duration of its life unless forcibly removed.

TREATING THE ENVIRONMENT AND THE DOG

Treating fleas should be a two-pronged attack. First, the environment needs to be treated; this includes carpets and furniture, especially the dog's bedding and

Opposite page: A scanning electron micrograph of a dog or cat flea, *Ctenocephalides*, magnified more than 100x. This image has been colourized for effect.

The Life Cycle of the Flea

Adult

Pupa

Larva

Egg

This graphic depiction of the life cycle of the flea appears courtesy of Fleabusters®, R_x for fleas.

areas underneath furniture. The environment should be treated with a household spray containing an Insect Growth Regulator (IGR) and an insecticide to kill the adult fleas. Most IGRs are effective against eggs and larvae; they actually mimic the fleas' own hormones and stop the eggs and larvae from developing into adult fleas. There are currently no treatments available to attack the pupa stage of the life cycle, so the adult insecticide is used to kill the newly hatched adult fleas before

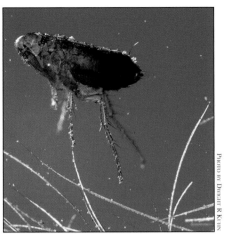

Photo by Dwight R Kuhn

TICKS AND MITES

Though not as common as fleas, ticks and mites are found all over the tropical and temperate world. They don't bite, like fleas; they harpoon. They dig their sharp proboscis (nose) into the dog's skin and drink the blood. Their only food and drink is dog's blood. Dogs can get Lyme disease, Rocky Mountain spotted fever (normally

Dwight R Kuhn's magnificent action photo showing a flea jumping from a dog's back.

they find a host. Most IGRs are active for many months, whilst adult insecticides are only active for a few days.

When treating with a household spray, it is a good idea to vacuum before applying the product. This stimulates as many pupae as possible to hatch into adult fleas. The vacuum cleaner should also be treated with a flea treatment to prevent the eggs and larvae that have been hoovered into the vacuum bag from hatching.

The second stage of treatment is to apply an adult insecticide to the dog. Traditionally, this would be in the form of a collar or a spray, but more recent innovations include digestible insecticides that poison the fleas when they ingest the dog's blood. Alternatively, there are drops that, when placed on the back of the animal's neck, spread throughout the fur and skin to kill adult fleas.

FLEA CONTROL

Two types of products should be used when treating fleas—a product to treat the pet and a product to treat the home. Adult fleas represent less than 1% of the flea population. The pre-adult fleas (eggs, larvae and pupae) represent more than 99% of the flea population and are found in the environment; it is in the case of pre-adult fleas that products containing an Insect Growth Regulator (IGR) should be used in the home.

IGRs are a new class of compounds used to prevent the development of insects. They do not kill the insect outright, but instead use the insect's biology against it to stop it from completing its growth. Products that contain methoprene are the world's first and leading IGRs. Used to control fleas and other insects, this type of IGR will stop flea larvae from developing and protect the house for up to seven months.

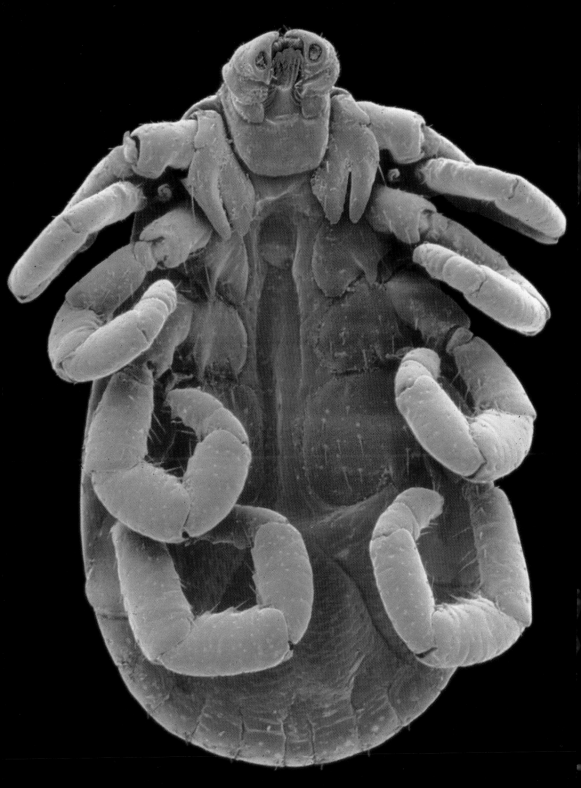

found in the US only), paralysis and many other diseases from ticks and mites. They may live where fleas are found and they like to hide in cracks or seams in walls wherever dogs live. They are controlled the same way fleas are controlled. The dog tick, *Dermacentor variabilis*, may well be the most common dog tick in many geographical areas, especially those areas where the climate is hot and humid.

Most dog ticks have life expectancies of a week to six

Beware the Deer Tick

The great outdoors may be fun for your dog, but it also is a home to dangerous ticks. Deer ticks carry a bacterium known as *Borrelia burgdorferi* and are most active in the autumn and spring. When infections are caught early, penicillin and tetracycline are effective antibiotics, but if left untreated the bacteria may cause neurological, kidney and cardiac problems as well as long-term trouble with walking and painful joints.

ILLUSTRATION COURTESY OF BAYER VITAL GMBH & CO. KG

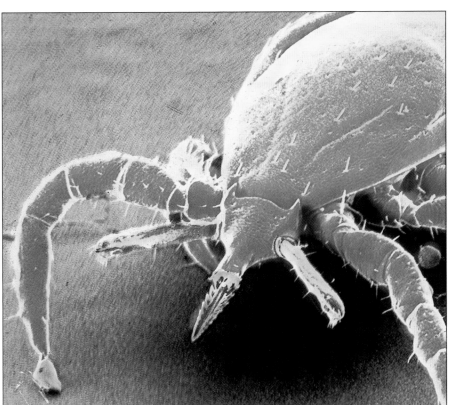

S. E. M. BY DR ANDREW SPIELMAN/PHOTOTAKE

A deer tick, the carrier of Lyme disease. This magnified micrograph has been colourized for effect.

Opposite page: The dog tick, *Dermacentor variabilis*, is probably the most common tick found on dogs. Look at the strength in its eight legs! No wonder it's hard to detach them.

139

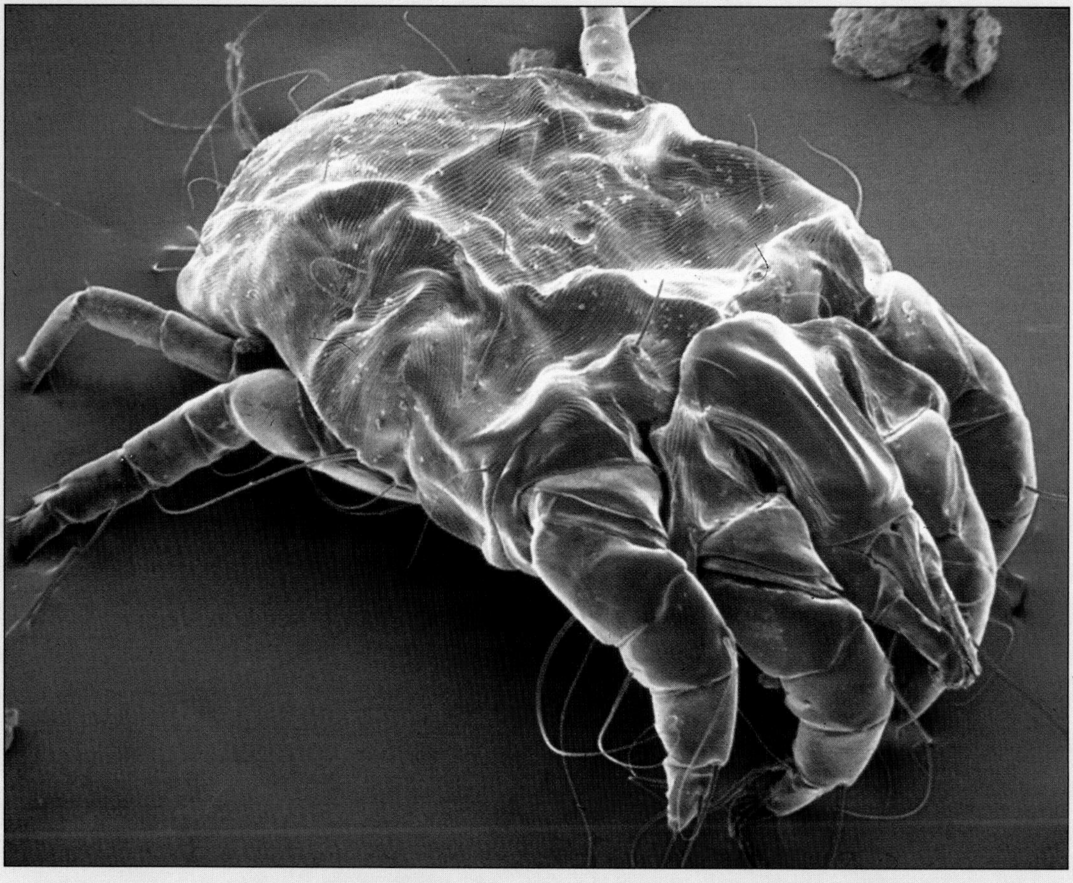

PHOTO BY JAMES HAYDEN-YOAW/PHOTOTAKE.

Above:
The mange mite, *Psoroptes bovis.*

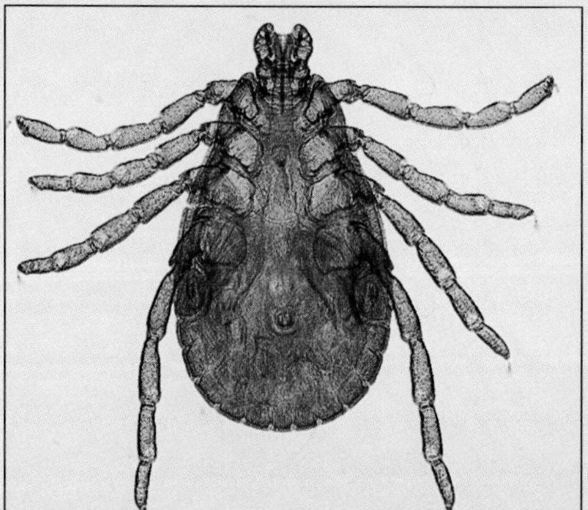

PHOTO BY CAROLINA BIOLOGICAL SUPPLY/PHOTOTAKE

A brown dog tick, *Rhipicephalus sanguineus*, is an uncommon but annoying tick found on dogs.

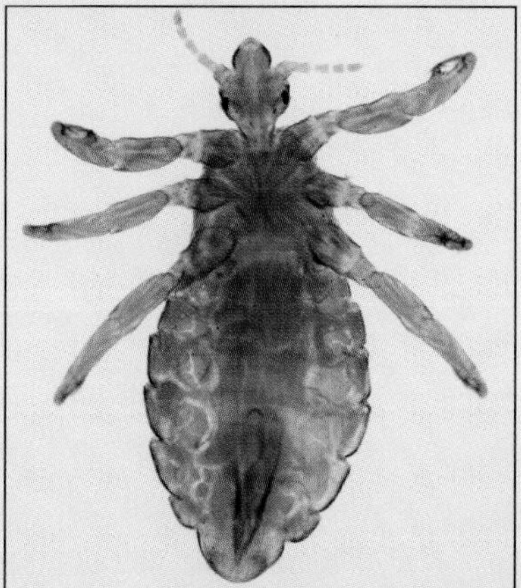

PHOTO BY DWIGHT R KUHN

Human lice look like dog lice; the two are closely related

months, depending upon climatic conditions. They can neither jump nor fly, but they can crawl slowly and can range up to 5 metres (16 feet) to reach a sleeping or unsuspecting dog.

MANGE

Mites cause a skin irritation called mange. Some are contagious, like *Cheyletiella*, ear mites, scabies and chiggers. Mites that cause ear-mite infestations are usually controlled with Lindane, which can only be administered by a vet, followed by Tresaderm at home.

It is essential that your dog be treated for mange as quickly as possible because some forms of mange are transmissible to people.

INTERNAL PARASITES

Most animals—fishes, birds and mammals, including dogs and humans—have worms and other parasites that live inside their bodies. According to Dr Herbert R Axelrod, the fish pathologist, there are two kinds of parasites: dumb and smart. The smart parasites live in peaceful cooper-ation with their hosts (symbiosis), while the dumb parasites kill their host. Most of the worm infections are relatively easy to control. If they are not controlled they weaken the host dog to the point that other medical problems occur, but they are not dumb parasites.

ROUNDWORMS

The roundworms that infect dogs are scientifically known as *Toxocara canis*. They live in the dog's intestine. The worms shed eggs continually. It has been estimated that a dog produces about 150 grammes of faeces every day. Each gramme of faeces averages 10,000–12,000 eggs of roundworms. There are no known areas in which dogs roam that do not contain roundworm eggs. The greatest danger of roundworms is that they infect people too! It is

DEWORMING

Ridding your puppy of worms is VERY IMPORTANT because certain worms that puppies carry, such as tapeworms and roundworms, can infect humans.

Breeders initiate a deworming programme at or about four weeks of age. The routine is repeated every two or three weeks until the puppy is three months old. The breeder from whom you obtained your puppy should provide you with the complete details of the deworming programme.

Your veterinary surgeon can prescribe and monitor the programme of deworming for you. The usual programme is treating the puppy every 15–20 days until the puppy is positively worm free.

It is not advised that you treat your puppy with drugs that are not recommended professionally.

wise to have your dog tested regularly for roundworms.

Pigs also have roundworm infections that can be passed to humans and dogs. The typical roundworm parasite is called *Ascaris lumbricoides*.

HOOKWORMS

The worm *Ancylostoma caninum* is commonly called the dog hookworm. It is dangerous to humans and cats. It also has teeth by which it attaches itself to the intestines of the dog. It changes the site of its attachment about six times a day and the dog loses blood from each detachment, possibly causing iron-deficiency anaemia. Hookworms are easily purged from the dog with many medications. Milbemycin oxime,

ROUNDWORMS

Average size dogs can pass 1,360,000 roundworm eggs every day.

For example, if there were only 1 million dogs in the world, the world would be saturated with 1,300 metric tonnes of dog faeces.

These faeces would contain 15,000,000,000 roundworm eggs.

It's known that 7–31% of home gardens and children's play boxes in the US contain roundworm eggs.

Flushing dog's faeces down the toilet is not a safe practice because the usual sewage treatments do not destroy roundworm eggs.

Infected puppies start shedding roundworm eggs at 3 weeks of age. They can be infected by their mother's milk.

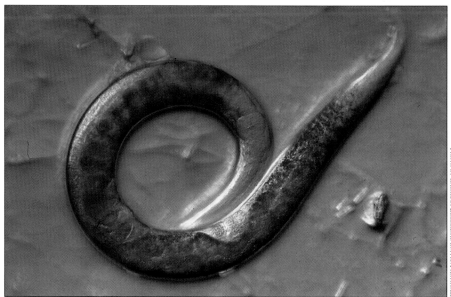

The roundworm, *Rhabditis*. The roundworm can infect both dogs and humans.

PHOTO BY CAROLINA BIOLOGICAL SUPPLY/PHOTOTAKE

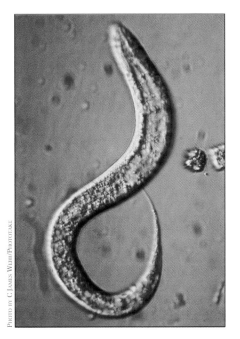

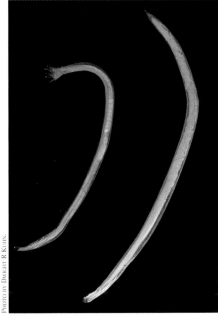

Left:
The infective stage of the hookworm larva.

Right:
Male and female hookworms, *Ancylostoma caninum*, are uncommonly found in pet or show dogs in Britain. Hookworms may infect other dogs that have exposure to grasslands.

which also serves as a heartworm preventative in Collies, can be used for this purpose.

In Britain the 'temperate climate' hookworm (*Uncinaria stenocephala*) is rarely found in pet or show dogs, but can occur in

---

DID YOU KNOW?

Never allow your dog to swim in polluted water or public areas where water quality can be suspect. Even perfectly clear water can harbour parasites, many of which can cause serious to fatal illnesses in canines. Areas inhabited by waterfowl and other wildlife are especially dangerous.

---

hunting packs, racing Greyhounds and sheepdogs because the worms can be prevalent wherever dogs are exercised regularly on grassland.

TAPEWORMS

There are many species of tapeworms. They are carried by fleas! The dog eats the flea and starts the tapeworm cycle. Humans can also be infected with tapeworms, so don't eat fleas! Fleas are so small that your dog could pass them onto your hands, your plate or your food and thus make it possible for you to ingest a flea which is carrying tapeworm eggs.

While tapeworm infection is not life threatening in dogs (smart parasite!), it can be the cause of a

143

The head and rostellum (the round prominence on the scolex) of a tapeworm, which infects dogs and humans.

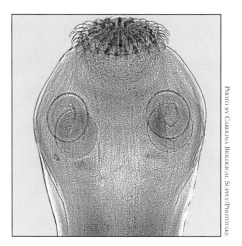

PHOTO BY CAROLINA BIOLOGICAL SUPPLY/PHOTOTAKE

TAPEWORMS

Humans, rats, squirrels, foxes, coyotes, wolves, mixed breeds of dogs and purebred dogs are all susceptible to tapeworm infection. Except in humans, tapeworms are usually not a fatal infection.

Infected individuals can harbour a thousand parasitic worms.

Tapeworms have two sexes—male and female (many other worms have only one sex—male and female in the same worm).

If dogs eat infected rats or mice, they get the tapeworm disease.

One month after attaching to a dog's intestine, the worm starts shedding eggs. These eggs are infective immediately.

Infective eggs can live for a few months without a host animal.

Roundworms, whipworms and hookworms are just a few of the other commonly known worms that infect dogs.

very serious liver disease for humans. About 50 percent of the humans infected with *Echinococcus multilocularis*, a type of tapeworm that causes alveolar hydatis, perish.

HEARTWORMS

Heartworms are thin, extended worms up to 30 cms (12 ins) long which live in a dog's heart and the major blood vessels surrounding it. Dogs may have up to 200 worms. Symptoms may be loss of energy, loss of appetite, coughing, the development of a pot belly and anaemia.

Heartworms are transmitted by mosquitoes. The mosquito drinks the blood of an infected dog and takes in larvae with the blood. The larvae, called microfilaria, develop within the body of the mosquito and are passed on to the next dog bitten after the larvae mature. It takes two to three weeks for the larvae to develop to the infective stage within the body of the mosquito. Dogs should be treated at about six weeks of age, and maintained on a prophylactic dose given monthly.

Blood testing for heartworms is not necessarily indicative of how seriously your dog is infected. This is a dangerous disease. Although heartworm is a problem for dogs in America, Australia, Asia and Central Europe, dogs in the United Kingdom are not currently affected by heartworm.

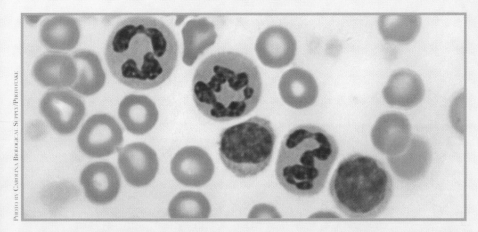

Magnified
heartworm
larvae,
*Dirofilaria
immitis.*

PHOTO BY CAROLINA BIOLOGICAL SUPPLY/PHOTOTAKE

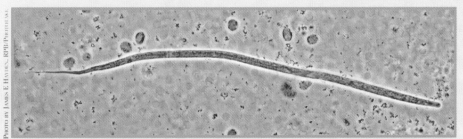

The heartworm,
Dirofilaria immitis.

PHOTO BY JAMES E HAYDEN, RPB/PHOTOTAKE

The heart
of a dog infected
with canine
heartworm,
*Dirofilaria
immitis.*

PHOTO BY JAMES E HAYDEN, RPB/PHOTOTAKE

145

DID YOU KNOW?

Earning a championship at Kennel Club shows is the most difficult in the world. Compared to the United States and Canada where it is

relatively not 'challenging,' collecting three green tickets not only requires much time and effort, it can be very expensive! Challenge Certificates, as the tickets are properly known, are the building blocks of champions—good breeding, good handling, good training and good luck!

When you purchased your Afghan Hound, you should have made it clear to the breeder whether you wanted one just as a loveable companion and pet, or if you hoped to be buying a Afghan Hound with show prospects. No reputable breeder will sell you a young puppy saying that it is *definitely* of show quality, for so much can go wrong during the early weeks and months of a puppy's development. If you plan to show, what you will hopefully have acquired is a puppy with 'show potential.'

To the novice, exhibiting an Afghan Hound in the show ring may look easy but it usually takes a lot of hard work and devotion to do top winning at a show such as the prestigious Crufts, not to mention a little luck too!

The first concept that the canine novice learns when watching a dog show is that each breed first competes against members of its own breed. Once the judge has selected the best member of each breed, provided that the show is judged on a Group system, that chosen dog will compete with other dogs in its group. Finally the best of each group will compete for Best in Show and Reserve Best in Show.

The second concept that you must understand is that the dogs are not actually competing against one another. The judge compares each dog against the breed standard, which is the written description of the ideal specimen of the breed. Whilst some early breed standards like the Afghan's were indeed based on specific dogs that were famous or popular, many dedicated enthusiasts say that a perfect specimen, described in the standard, has never been bred. Thus, the 'perfect' dog never walked into a show ring, has never been bred and, to the woe of dog breeders around the globe, does not exist. Breeders attempt to get as close to this ideal as possible with every litter, but theoretically the 'perfect' dog is so elusive that it is impossible (and if the 'perfect' dog were born, breeders and judges would never agree that it was indeed 'perfect').

If you are interested in exploring dog shows, your best bet is to join your local breed club. These clubs often host both Championship and Open Shows, and sometimes Match meetings and Special Events, all of which

could be of interest, even if you are only an onlooker. Clubs also send out newsletters and some organise training days and seminars in order that people may learn more about their chosen breed. To locate the

CLASSES AT DOG SHOWS

There can be as many as 18 classes per sex for your breed. Check the show schedule carefully to make sure that you have entered your dog in the appropriate class. Among the classes offered can be:

Beginners; Minor Puppy (ages 6 to 9 months); Puppy (ages 6 to 12 months); Junior (ages 6 to 18 months); Beginners (handler or dog never won first place) as well as the following, each of which is defined in the schedule: Maiden; Novice; Tyro; Debutant; Undergraduate; Graduate; Postgraduate; Minor Limit; Mid Limit; Limit; Open; Veteran; Stud Dog; Brood Bitch; Progeny; Brace and Team.

DID YOU KNOW?

There are 330 breeds recognised by the FCI, and each breed is considered to be 'owned' by a specific country. Each breed standard is a cooperative effort between the breed's country and the FCI's Standards and Scientific Commissions. Judges use these official breed standards at shows held in FCI member countries. One of the functions of the FCI is to update and translate the breed standards into French, English, Spanish and German.

nearest breed club for you, contact The Kennel Club, the ruling body for the British dog world. The Kennel Club governs not only conformation shows but also working trials, obedience trials, agility trials and field trials. The Kennel Club furnishes the rules and regulations for all these events plus general dog registration and other basic requirements of dog ownership. Its annual show called the Crufts Dog Show, held in Birmingham, is the largest benched show in England. Every year around 20,000 of the UK's best dogs qualify to participate in this marvellous show which lasts four days.

The Kennel Club governs many different kinds of shows. At the most competitive and prestigious of these shows, the Championship Shows, a dog can earn Challenge Certificates, and thereby become a Show Champion or a Champion. A dog must earn three Challenge Certificates under three different judges to earn the prefix of 'Sh Ch' or 'Ch.' Note that some breeds must also qualify in a field trial in order to gain the title of full champion. Challenge Certificates are awarded to a very small percentage of the dogs competing, especially as dogs which are already Champions compete with others for these coveted CCs. The number of Challenge Certificates awarded in any one year is based upon the total number of dogs in each breed entered for competition. There are three types of Championship Shows: an all-breed General Championship show for all Kennel-Club-recognised breeds; a Group Championship Show, limited to breeds within one of the groups; and a Breed Show, usually confined to a single breed. The Kennel Club determines which breeds at which Championship Shows will have the opportunity to earn Challenge Certificates (or 'tickets'). Serious exhibitors often will opt not to participate if the tickets are withheld at a particular show. This policy makes earning championships even more difficult to

It is a common sight to see contestants giving their Afghans a last-minute brushing before their appearance in the ring.

DID YOU KNOW?

The FCI *does not* issue pedigrees. The FCI members and contract partners are responsible for issuing pedigrees and training judges in their own countries. The FCI does maintain a list of judges and makes sure that they are recognised throughout the FCI member countries.

The FCI also *does not* act as a breeder referral; breeder information is available from FCI-recognised national canine societies in each of the FCI's member countries.

accomplish.

Open Shows are generally less competitive and are frequently used as 'practice shows' for young dogs. There are hundreds of Open Shows each year that can be invitingly social events and are great first show experiences for the novice. Even if you're considering just watching a show to wet your paws, an Open Show is a great choice.

Whilst Championship and Open Shows are most important for the beginner to understand,

149

DID YOU KNOW?

FCI-recognised breeds are divided into ten groups:

Group 1: Sheepdogs and Cattledogs (except Swiss Cattledogs)

Group 2: Pinschers and Schnauzers, Molossians, Swiss Mountain Dogs and Swiss Cattledogs

Group 3: Terriers

Group 4: Dachshunds

Group 5: Spitz- and primitive-type dogs

Group 6: Scenthounds and related breeds

Group 7: Pointing dogs

Group 8: Retrievers, Flushing dogs and Water dogs

Group 9: Companion and Toy dogs

Group 10: Sighthounds

there are other types of shows in which the interested dog owner can participate. Training clubs sponsor Matches that can be entered on the day of the show for a nominal fee. In these introductory-level exhibitions, two dogs are pulled out of a hat and 'matched,' the winner of that match goes on to the next round and eventually only one dog is left undefeated.

Exemption Shows are much more light-hearted affairs with usually only four pedigree classes and several 'fun' classes, all of which can be entered on the day. The proceeds of an Exemption Show must be given to a charity. These shows are sometimes held in conjunction with small agricultural shows. Limited Shows are also available in small number, but entry is restricted to members of the club which hosts the show, although one can usually join the club when making an entry.

Before you actually step into the ring, you would be well advised to sit back and observe the judge's ring procedure. If it is your first time in the ring, do not be over-anxious and run to the front of the line. It is much better to stand back and study how the exhibitor in front of you is performing. The judge asks each handler to 'stand' the dog, hopefully showing the dog off to his best advantage. The judge will observe the dog from a distance and from different angles, approach the dog and check his teeth, overall structure, alertness and muscle tone, as well as consider how well the dog 'conforms' to the standard. Most importantly, the judge will have the exhibitor move the dog around the ring in some pattern that he or she should specify (another advantage to not going first, but always listen since some judges change their directions, and the judge is always right!). Finally, the judge will give the dog one last look before moving on to the next exhibitor.

If you are not in the top three at your first show, do not be discouraged. Be patient and consistent and you may eventually find yourself in the winning lineup. Remember that the winners were once in your shoes and have devoted many hours and much money to earn the placement. If you find that your dog is losing every time and never getting a nod, it may be time to consider a different dog sport or just enjoy your Afghan Hound as a pet.

An Afghan's gait is an important physical trait that is evaluated by the judge.

WORKING TRIALS

Working trials can be entered by any well-trained dog of any breed, not just Gundogs or Working dogs. Many dogs that earn the Kennel Club Good Citizen Dog award choose to participate in a working trial. There are five stakes at both open and championship levels: Companion Dog (CD), Utility Dog (UD), Working Dog (WD), Tracking Dog (TD) and Patrol Dog (PD). As in conformation shows, dogs compete against a standard and if the dog reaches the qualifying mark, it obtains a certificate. Divided into groups,

each exercise must be achieved 70 percent in order to qualify. If the dog achieves 80 percent in the open level, it receives a Certificate of Merit (COM); in the championship level, it receives a Qualifying Certificate. At the CD stake, dogs must participate in four groups: Control, Stay, Agility and Search (Retrieve and Nosework). At the next three levels: UD, WD and TD, there are only three groups: Control, Agility and Nosework.

Agility consists of three jumps: a vertical scale up a six-foot wall of planks; a clear jump over a basic three-foot hurdle

An Afghan Hounds must first compete against members of its own breed before advancing to Group and Best in Show competition.

with a removable top bar; and a long jump across angled planks stretching nine feet.

To earn the UD, WD and TD, dogs must track approximately one-half mile for articles laid from one-half hour to three hours before. Tracks consist of turns and legs, and fresh ground is used for each participant.

The fifth stake, PD, involves teaching manwork, which is not recommended for every breed.

FIELD TRIALS AND WORKING TESTS

Working tests are frequently used to prepare dogs for field trials, the purpose of which is to heighten the instincts and natural abilities of gundogs. Live game is not used in working tests. Unlike field trials, working tests do not count toward a dog's record at The Kennel Club, though the same judges often oversee working tests. Field trials began in England in 1947 and are only moderately popular amongst dog folk. Whilst breeders of Working and Gundog breeds concern themselves with the field abilities of their dogs, there is considerably less interest in field trials than dog shows. In order for dogs to become full champions, certain breeds must qualify in the field as well. Upon gaining three CCs in the show ring, the dog is designated a Show Champion (Sh Ch). The

SHOW RING ETIQUETTE

Just as with anything else, there is a certain etiquette to the show ring that can only be learned through experience. Showing your dog can be quite intimidating to you as a novice when it seems as if everyone else knows what they are doing. You can familiarise yourself with ring procedure beforehand by taking a class to prepare you and your dog for conformation showing or by talking with an experienced handler. When you are in the ring, listen and pay attention to the judge and follow his/her directions. Remember, even the most skilled handlers had to start somewhere. Keep it up and you too will become a proficient handler before too long!

title Champion (Ch) requires that the dog gain an award at a field trial, be a 'special qualifier' at a field trial or pass a 'special show dog qualifier' judged by a field trial judge on a shooting day.

AGILITY TRIALS

Agility trials began in the United Kingdom in 1977 and have since spread around the world, especially to the United States, where the sport enjoys strong popularity. The handler directs his dog over an obstacle course that includes jumps (such as those used in the working trials), as well as tyres, the dog walk, weave poles, pipe tunnels, collapsed tunnels, etc. The Kennel Club requires that dogs not be trained for agility until they are 12 months old. This dog sport intends to be great fun for dog and owner and interested owners should join a training club that has obstacles and experienced agility handlers who can introduce you and your dog to the 'ropes' (and tyres, tunnels and so on).

FÉDÉRATION CYNOLOGIQUE INTERNATIONALE

Established in 1911, the Fédération Cynologique Internationale (FCI) represents the 'world kennel club.' This international body brings uniformity to the breeding, judging and showing of purebred dogs. Although the FCI originally included only five European nations: France, Germany, Austria, Netherlands and Belgium (which remains its headquarters), the organisation today embraces nations on six continents and recognises well over 300 breeds of purebred dog. There are three titles attainable through the FCI: the International Champion, which is the most prestigious; the International Beauty Champion, which is based on aptitude certificates in different countries; and the International Trial Champion,

which is based on achievement in obedience trials in different countries. Dogs from around the world participate in these impressive FCI spectacles, the largest of which is the World Dog Show, hosted in a different country each year. FCI sponsors both national and international shows. The hosting country determines the judging system and breed standards are always based on the breed's country of origin.

The FCI is divided into ten 'Groups.' At the World Dog Show, the following 'Classes' are offered for each breed: Puppy Class (6–9 months), Youth Class (9–18 months), Open Class (15 months or older) and Champion Class. A dog can be awarded a classification of Excellent, Very Good, Good, Sufficient and Not Sufficient. Puppies can be awarded classifications of Very Promising, Promising or Not Promising. Four placements are made in each class. After all sexes and classes are judged, a Best of Breed is selected. Other special groups and classes may also be shown. Each exhibitor showing a dog receives a written evaluation from the judge.

Besides the World Dog Show, you can exhibit your dog at speciality shows held by different breed clubs. Speciality shows may have their own regulations.

Conformation is not the only type of competition in which the Afghan can participate. Afghans and their owners also enjoy more breed-specific competition such as racing and lure coursing.

INDEX

*Page numbers in **boldface** indicate illustrations.*

My Afghan Hound

PUT YOUR PUPPY'S FIRST PICTURE HERE

Dog's Name _____

Date _____ Photographer _____